The Art of SERIES

EDITED BY CHARLES BAXTER

The Art of series is a line of books reinvigorating the practice of craft and criticism. Each book is a brief, witty, and useful exploration of fiction, nonfiction, or poetry by a writer impassioned by a singular craft issue. *The Art of* volumes provide a series of sustained examinations of key, but sometimes neglected, aspects of creative writing by some of contemporary literature's finest practitioners.

THE ART OF
RECKLESSNESS

POETRY AS ASSERTIVE FORCE
AND CONTRADICTION

The Art of

RECKLESSNESS

POETRY AS ASSERTIVE FORCE
AND CONTRADICTION

Dean Young

Graywolf Press

Portions of this book appeared in various forms in *American Poetry, Poetry,* and *Poets & Writers.*

This publication is made possible by funding provided in part by a grant from the Minnesota State Arts Board, through an appropriation by the Minnesota State Legislature, a grant from the National Endowment for the Arts, and private funders. Significant support has also been provided by Target; the McKnight Foundation; and other generous contributions from foundations, corporations, and individuals. To these organizations and individuals we offer our heartfelt thanks.

NATIONAL ENDOWMENT FOR THE ARTS

MINNESOTA STATE ARTS BOARD

WELLS FARGO

TARGET.

Published by Graywolf Press
250 Third Avenue North, Suite 600
Minneapolis, Minnesota 55401
All rights reserved.

www.graywolfpress.org

Published in the United States of America

ISBN 978-1-55597-562-3

4 6 8 9 7 5 3

Library of Congress Control Number: 2010920768

Cover design: Scott Sorenson

Author acknowledgments
Thanks to Charlie Baxter for asking me to contribute to this series. Enormous gratitude to Cornelia Nixon, who nudged this much closer to a recognizable language.

For Ellen Bryant Voigt,
who encouraged me to think
(it's not her fault what *I thought)*
& Donald Revell

A. A violent order is disorder; and

B. A great disorder is an order. These

Two things are one. (Pages of illustrations.)

—Wallace Stevens, "Connoisseur of Chaos"

You'll never catch a fish

that way, you said. One caught a fish that way.

—Robert Hass, "Berkeley Eclogue"

RECKLESSNESS

POETRY AS ASSERTIVE FORCE
AND CONTRADICTION

Let us suppose that everyone in the world wakes up today and tries to write a poem. It is impossible to know what will happen next but certainly we may be assured that the world will not be made worse. I believe in the divinity of profligacy. The creation of art, okay, just the attempt at the creation of art, as well as the appreciation of it, is both an enlarging of the world and an expanding of consciousness. To write a poem is to explore the unknown capacities of the mind and the heart; it is emotive, empathetic exercise and, like being struck by lightning, it will probably leave you stunned, singed, but also a bit brighter, and too your odds of being struck again then go much higher. Sometimes when we feel disappointed with a poem, with our effort, feel that the poem fails us, it's because it seems to fall short of our intentions. But those intentions are often vague and speculative, and any attempted actualization of those ideas can't help but be anemic. Let us forgive ourselves for writing poems that aren't better than every other poem that has ever been written. The nagging sense of failure may not be that the poem falls short but rather that the forms of intention are themselves at fault, producing a too-ready verdict

*writing poetry requires equal parts discipline and recklessness

of failure. Prescription may offer a kind of security; it presupposes, provides a certainty based on very little before engaging something that is not even there yet. No one knows how to write a poem. Congratulations! Prescription and intention are traps. They promise a certainty of outcome, of identifiability based upon acquired skills that can only be parroted back at best. To approach the practice of poetry as an acquiring of skill sets may provide the stability of a curriculum, but the source of inspiration is as much instability, recklessness. Poets are excellent students of blizzards and salt and broken statuary, but they are always elsewhere for the test. Any intention in the writing of poetry beyond the most basic aim to make a poem, of engaging the materials, SHOULD be disappointed. If the poet does not have the chutzpah to jeopardize habituated assumptions and practices, what will be produced will be sleep without dream, a copy of a copy of a copy. The poem always intends otherwise. At every moment the poet must be ready to abandon any prior intention in welcome expectation of what the poem is beginning to signal. More than intending, the poet ATTENDS! Attends to the conspiracy of words as it reveals itself as a poem, to its murmurs of radiant content that may be encouraged to shout, to its muffled musics there to be discovered and conducted. Revision is just that, and it begins before the first word is even written; it is not some activity done on Tuesdays and Thursdays while

poetry is present, prioritize the life within your own words

ATTEND TO LANGUAGE

freewriting, surely a governmental phrase, is done on Mondays and Wednesdays. It is and needs to be a messy process, a devotion to unpredictability, the papers blowing around the room as the wind comes in.

Let us put to rest all those huffy complaints about the proliferation of MFA programs, as if courses of study that offer support and allowance to people for the exploration of their inner lives, for the respected regard of their imaginations, their harmless madnesses and idiosyncratic musics and wild surmises, somehow lead to a great homogeneity as well as a great dilution of the high principles of art. Some people try to convince you they love poetry by showing you how bad all the poetry they read (more likely don't read) is, just like those who love love so much they've come to the conclusion that nothing and no one deserve to be loved. Some people try to convince you poetry is so important you have no business trying to write it without severe indoctrination. But POETRY CAN'T BE HARMED BY PEOPLE TRYING TO WRITE IT! The billions of MFA programs and community creative writing workshops and summer conferences and readings, all of it is a great sign of health, that the imaginative life is thriving and important, and worthy of time and attention, worthy of conditions in which it is honored and encouraged to wildly grow. It's not a marketplace where the bad forces out the good. We are not a consumer group; we are a tribe. The MFA programs may be booming because our business is to boom. OUR BUSINESS IS BLOOMING. If there is a problem, it is in the professionalization of creative writing. J'accuse, AWP! When Tomaž Šalamun was asked by one of my students what was the one thing he would like to tell a young poet, he said, Be artists, not careerists. I do realize that people have real economic concerns, and two or three years of graduate study are traditionally geared toward the establishment of a career. But realistically, all these young writers cannot be English professors, nor do many of them actually want to be. Our creative writing programs could do a better job offering students guidance in other possible employment options, suggesting courses, outside creative writing and literature that could lead them to decent work outside academe. But when I walk into a creative writing class of any kind, I am thrilled with the liberty that all of us in that room have managed to achieve through a faith in and dedication to art, and the profound sense of possibility that something one of us does can become a vibrant part of that art.

THE ERROR IS NOT TO FALL BUT TO FALL FROM NO HEIGHT

To be interested in poetry is not so much to be interested in a thing like sodium or statuary. Poetry occurs between primaries, the page and the mind, the world and the word. More than a thing, it is a transference of energy between poles. Poetry's task, if it has one (we must be suspicious of any claim of task), IS to mitigate but to mitigate by way of accelerant: it too becomes primary in a range from rivaling the world to near exclusion and/or creation of it, to a humble transparency that adds nothing but clarity, the way a very clean window can add luster to a gray day it looks out on and frames. Some impurities can make water clearer.

Poetry is no more a thing than fire is; rather it is a conversion that reveals itself in the instance of its occasion. Poetry mitigates just as fire does, by witnessing its own necessary recklessness and senses of the sacred, its ability to combust the ancillary, to grow and make everything itself even as it confronts us with the outcome of its conjugations, with ash, with death. Let us not forget that the punishment for the god who gave us fire in a hollow reed (already fire was singing) is eternal evisceration. Aesthetic positions are often drawn toward their own extinction, be it through the impossibilities of their aims or the ruination brought about by their success. Romantic transcendence incorporated its own failure in order to continue; dada made central to itself not only its own failure but the failure of any other artistic position and expression; surrealism posited a utopic position that was not interested in the production of literary artifacts, as André Breton said, but rather the use of poetic/artistic processes to accomplish the ruination of a shackled intellect and the liberation of another kind of mind. In the case of art that defines itself as resistance, its continued effectiveness is dependent upon the continued health of that which it resists, just as the vitality of a virus depends upon the continued survival of its host. (Viruses, as we know, may be ingenious but they're rather dumb and often polish off their hosts, the definition of a bad houseguest.) Once that critique has been assimilated or worn out, it becomes defanged, domesticated, no longer combative, rather quaint. Quaintness may be the worst that can happen to an art, its fire replaced by a lava lamp. The worst thing that can happen to an artist is to become a bore, to become complacent.

To cultivate fire is to perpetually gather fuel, sometimes to reconceive what IS fuel. While poetry perpetually examines its own means, it must also move outside itself else it burn pale, offer only a redundant twilight on a cloudy day, giving illumination in too narrow a spectrum. Perhaps it is appealing to become involved with the complexities of an unreliable symbolic medium purely to make a poetry that demonstrates a diverting befuddlement of scattered signs that leave a trail from nowhere to nowhere, that remain busily static in the labyrinth. But I don't think so. Literary theory (reader, you can sleep through this part if you want), along with its successes, particularly in refreshing forms of self-awareness, has managed, through powerful critique arising from a consideration of writing as a mode of cultural commodification embedded in often patriarchal, late capitalist, racist biases and/or the very shifty unintelligibility of signs *(zzzzz),* to make us see authorial intention as a form of molestation and indoctrination or to see the author as merely responding to social pressures like a squeezed rubber duck and the poem is its squeak. Literature at best, in these terms, can aspire to free play among constructs, an anarchy that undercuts any reverence for meaning and any desire for meaning becomes a perverse need, an appeal for an authority by a weak mind.

THE BLOOD MAY BE FAKE BUT THE BLEEDING MUST BE REAL

"Blood" may only be used for its rhyming with "mud," as Viktor Shklovsky says. We have no choice but to acknowledge the artificiality of our means, the construct of language, the artifice of any poem as a series of literary devices. Yet what we must acknowledge we must also override, we must destabilize and hoist the ironized bits of the dismembered literary corpses, the literary devices we've sown together, into the thunderstorm and sometimes LIGHTNING the monster lives! When I cut myself, it's not a construct that bleeds.

This poststructuralist critique has lent vitality to poetry that tends to counter and consume it, has expanded modes of expressivity beyond the descriptive/image-driven and rational discursive through a suspicion of habituated poetic modes of expression and of the shaping of both worldly and aesthetic experience. The finishing off of literature has always been a great help to literature. Mallarmé wrote a poem to end all poems with "A Throw of the Dice," as if any single instance of chance could abolish chance. Whitman unleashed a virus that threatened to make everything a Whitman poem, or at least a part of the Whitman Sampler. Even as equivocating a poet as John Ashbery, through the prolific and tangential profusion of his work, seemed for a time to be threatening to destroy the distinction between what was and wasn't poetry. (There is no more exquisite, lively, and welcoming body of work in poetry than what Ashbery continues to give us, none more world enlarging.) Poetry always needs more fuel, different fuel. For every time poetry has consumed itself, it has managed to turn up elsewhere, incendiary, primitive, unable to be snuffed out. The monster lives!

As much as by way of claims of power, poetry continues to ignite because of its renewed humiliation and reductions, the stripping of its armor (the first thing Apollo did to Patroklos when Patroklos thought he was really hot shit was knock his helmet off). In witnessing its own burial, poetry chafes up its primary spark, its basic principles and drives, its basic and fundamental centrality to the human dilemma, both in representing it as subject but also as site from which poetry comes, its occasion. Poetry is a manifestation of the spirit as it triangulates itself through the desires and limitations of meat, meditative inklings of immortality, and the play in the manipulation of aestheticized materials. It forgets about itself as code making, has the supreme confidence of handling elemental fuels. The word then is not only fit referent but also magical embodiment of the thing, the word takes its flesh from the world. Transubstantiation. The names of the dead are not to be trifled with. Forgiveness is asked for. And power. And self. We have arrived at the primitive.

Before we became obligated only to our minds, we were obligated to the world, its bodied conception and celebration and morning. Our poems are what the gods couldn't make without going through us. We were answering back, not making codes, not manipulating literary devices, but offering thanks and accusation, mimicries of fundamental mysteries, the simplicities of urges that are always with us in the language of the creature, experience, weather. Our poetry is our haunting and adventure.

"Say you think life is trembling," wrote Willem de Kooning of an idea he picked up in Kierkegaard. "Pretty soon everything trembles. Raphael trembles. Poussin trembles." De Kooning's point is that it doesn't matter so much what you think as you think it with a conviction that arises from the closely observed and considered world itself. I'm asking you here to consider poetry that is unhindered by doubt (while acknowledging that doubt can begin the inspiration toward liberation), a poetry that arises out of recklessness and is composed of convictions of first needs, first minds, of truth in language arising from the active impulse of emotion, moving through the calculations of the rational toward irrational detonation.

By the primitive I mean exploration of primary human dilemmas, the assertion of the monstrous if need be, the instinctual, visceral, sexual, rogue, absurd, sometimes derangement as a form of innocence. Primary even in afterness. Not ironic.

> "It is necessary to any originality to have the courage to be an amateur."
>
> —Wallace Stevens

I ask you as a poet, reader, to always remember your first urges, why you wrote your first poem. Everyone is a wonderful poet up until the third grade. I saw it when I taught as a poet in the schools. The sublime coincides with the ridiculous, babble with referent, the witnessed phenomena with the combustion of name in song of dazzling appeal, of play. The alphabet presents itself as an unsolvable mystery to be frolicked in. Words themselves create reality through music and incantation: "One fish, two fish, red fish, blue fish." The profligacies of rhyme, its irrationalities bring forth new realities. The world arises from naming and naming itself is a product of hilarity, invention, fortuitous accident, the elsewhere and elsewhat and elsewho, the imagination. So too darkness, the sense of desertion, profound isolation, inadequacy, that you will never be loved enough no not ever, connect us to the primary wellsprings of poetry as children. Same as now.

Having a conversation with a couple of dreary poets a while back, I lamented how little the imagination is referred to in discussions of the merits of poetry and one said she felt the imagination played no part in her work because she certainly wouldn't want it thought of as imaginary. "Oh Imagination," proclaims Wordsworth in *The Prelude* after crossing the Alps but missing the peak, the peak experience in fog. The imagination plays as

[in life]

much a part in the creation of reality as it does in the confections of the false, "the whims of imagination . . . alone [cause] real things" (Breton). It is what we appeal to and rely on when our empirical data has proved insufficient to the case. THE HIGHEST ACCOMPLISHMENT OF HUMAN CONSCIOUSNESS IS THE IMAGINATION AND THE HIGHEST ACCOMPLISHMENT OF THE IMAGINATION IS EMPATHY and the ability to love, and if you don't think that takes a profound part in the creation of the world, please close this book right now.

So what happens? When kids hit the fourth grade: socialization. Maturation. Kids begin feeling immense pressure to conform and conceal, accept responsibility and obligation, expect punishment, fear being ostracized, shunned from the herd. This shows up quickly in their writing. Unicorns everywhere, the same unicorn, commodification of the mythic as well as sexual. Adjectives restricted to training wheels. The external life, which previously was presented as collaborative experience between the world, the self, and the world-making words, becomes slave to etiquette and fashion. The emotional life becomes circumscribed, repressed. We learn, for the best in general I suppose, to control ourselves even as the onslaught of sexual imperative begins to scramble our wits (it will never stop) and our spirit goes deeper and deeper into hiding (definitely not for the good). Civilization makes us ill. An exploratory experience is turned into a hall pass.

> "How sad it is when a luxurious imagination is obliged in self defense to deaden its delicacy in vulgarity, and riot in things attainable that it may not have leisure to go mad after things that are not."
>
> —John Keats, 7 July 1818

Let us riot in the unattainable!

Poetry is when the animal bursts forth, inflamed. It ain't always pretty. We are permitted to say everything is possible, brief consolation for what we've taken that we don't want and what we should have taken but were too afraid, proud, or stupid to. We can't have everything.

In *Looking for Spinoza,* the neurologist Antonio Damasio writes, "Organisms naturally endeavor, of necessity, to persevere in their own being." How we tell the difference between a thing that is alive and a thing that isn't is through its "drives, motivations, emotions, feelings," in a word, its affect. Affect is the fire, it is what moves. Within the symbolic medium of poetry, affect may reveal itself as a challenge to the medium's regularity, its conventions, but that challenge is most effective when it reveals motivation. It is through the trace of affect that we feel whether a poem is living, smack dab in the human dilemma, or dead. Poetry must assert itself as poetry. Emotion is our greatest primary affectual mode, moving from recollections in tranquillity to meditations in emergency, and to speak of emotion as a noun is misleading. It is a verb: feeling, constantly moving, negotiating between the obligation to and liberty from the world, the medium, and instinctual biological as well as philosophical need. Feeling. The preservation of being is an imaginative act.

"It is difficult to say for what reason the very things that move our senses most to pleasures and appeal to them most speedily at first are the ones from which we are most quickly estranged by a kind of disgust and surfeit. How much more brilliant, as a rule, in beauty and variety of coloring are new pictures compared to the old ones. But though they captivate us at first sight the pleasure does not last, while the very roughness and crudity of old painting maintains their hold on us." E. M. Gombrich begins his study, *Preference for the Primitive*, with this quote from Cicero to argue that Cicero's sense of "the passage from gratification to disgust" leads to a renewing primitivism, an avoidance reaction to the intellectual complexities and hierophantic codings, away from elegance toward a more basic, immediate, even brutal artistic expression and practice. The movement

between high finish and rough surface, between the in-
formed rigors of technique and the rash slash has been
a constant fluctuation throughout culture's history.

In the seventeenth century, imports from Korea, China,
and southern Asia made the Japanese tea ceremony
an occasion for ostentatious display of conspicuous
consumption. Sen no Rikyu, through his devotion to
zen principles, opposed such luxury by insisting on
principles of wabi-sabi. "The art of cha-no-yu con-
sists in nothing else but in boiling water, making tea,
and sipping it," Rikyu stated. Using much more basic,
homespun, cruder materials, his devotion to purity,
simplicity, even poverty, had repercussions throughout
Japanese culture. Rikyu, a celebrity and friend of the
emperor, was the man to impress. One tea man, who
owned a caddy in a special pattern, smashed it when
Rikyu acted as if he hadn't noticed it. A friend of the
owner later collected the pieces and glued them together
and invited Rikyu to see if he would notice the repaired
caddy. When served, Rikyu said, recognizing it, "When
it is repaired like this, it has really turned into a piece of
wabi." "It's better with the cracks," Duchamp would say
nearly three centuries later when his large glass, *The
Bride Stripped Bare by Her Bachelors, Even* on which he
worked, if we can use that word for Duchamp's whim-
sical, lazy process, for years, was smashed in storage.

Ironically, the restored teapot then became quite valuable and prized, sold for over 100,000 yen. Rikyu would be asked to commit suicide by his emperor, Hideyoshi, in part for the disruption caused by his growing insistence on humility and austerity.

For Western culture, the movement toward/return to the primitive is lastingly vigorous from the early twentieth century on. Beginning in painting but extending into literature, music, and dance, the artist turned from mastery of illusion and technique to a more unmitigated, raw relationship with the basic materials of the medium, and, at times, a spiritual even mythological assertion of the rights and peril of the artist and humankind. The artist then attempts to establish a primacy of intention through activity that removes itself from an established precedence of demonstrated expertise and turns toward/back to barer, harsher, more directly expressive modes.

Started in 1906 and finished, although Picasso never regarded it as complete, completion itself being called into question by the primitive, in 1907, *Les Demoiselles d'Avignon* takes as inspiration the crude force of African statuettes and masks. Certainly building on Cézanne's geometric deformation and destructions of the human figure, Picasso slashes the wild shapes, cones, cylinders, angles, and curves that both describe and obliterate realism while recalling tribal scarring. The interest in Oceanic and African art was shared by many of Picasso's contemporaries, and its mysterious, even biological force, stands in contrast to the aridity of cubism while nonetheless informing it. Picasso had pilfered quite a collection of primitive objects from the Louvre for inspiration that he would subsequently throw into the Seine when his friend Apollinaire, whom he would deny knowing in court, was arrested for stealing the *Mona Lisa.*

In *Les Demoiselles* there is an insistence upon physicality in the harsh coloration and jagged line. The brush strokes convey a savagery, a hacking that threatens to destroy what it depicts so that the act of depiction becomes emotive, not an illusion but a desecration, something that happens. "When he began to parody black art, he was stating what no eighteenth-century artist would have ever imagined suggesting: that the tradition of the human figure, which had been the very spine of Western art for two and a half millennia, had at last run out; and that in order to renew its vitality, one had to look to untapped cultural resources—the Africans, remote in their otherness," writes Robert Hughes in *The Shock of the New.* Picasso's access to these materials and use of them are implicated in the nineteenth-century French empire in equatorial Africa that imported these artifacts as cultural curiosity and booty but with no regard for them as art. But the exploitation of the artist and that of empire are very different, and to condemn both in the same terms, as if the co-opting of forms and procedures is the same as the subjugation, suppression, and enslavement of peoples, is to refuse the search for otherness in art (which rejuvenates it and creates humane connection) and would enforce a kind of quarantine and suffocation upon the artist. The imagination is about the business of empathetic rearticulating of the foreign, the strange, the other.

In its "attack on the eye" as Hughes calls it, reminding us of another famous attack on the eye that begins *An Andalusian Dog, Les Demoiselles,* while being an unmistakable echo of the three graces, a favored image of the late Renaissance, shoves aside perspective and conventional modes of the creation of volume and shadow to convey depth in favor of frontal exposure that to this day seems alarmingly naked, the nudity of whores not gods, cracked and fallen brides stripped bare. But these women are not subjugated; they are powerful, devoid of apology or flirtation in a morphological realization of the glare of Manet's *Olympia.* Sexual energy, direct, confrontational, even scary, is one of the volcanic wellsprings of the primitive.

In *The Pleasure of the Text,* Roland Barthes writes, "Is not the most erotic portion of the body *where the gar-*

ment gapes?" Our attention is drawn toward "the intermittence of skin flashing between two articles of clothing . . . between two edges . . . it is this flash itself which seduces." Our attention is magnetized by the gap, and it is in this gap, the glimpses it allows, that our attention is eroticized, pleasured. In many ways this gap seems to be where deconstruction sticks its snout, the disjunction between sign and referent, between word and thing that germinates both a proliferation of signs, a free play as well as an exhaustion, a forever falling short and perpetual deferring of the consummation of meaning. But desire, the motivating force, is kept in play. Only through this deferral is the end stop of meaning dodged. Desire vanishes at the point of capture, of attainment, the goal of the mind's penetration.

One of the greatest technicians of desire was also one of the most ironic: Duchamp; much of his work can be seen as forms of keep-away, electing and befuddling the viewer's drive toward attainment, toward verifiability, a frustration he called "delay." This notion of delay, he has said, began while he was looking in a shop window at a chocolate grinder (and in the hermeneutic lexicon of Duchamp, the mechanized grinder as eroticized object and the window or glass receive many reiterations). What he realized was that the desire he felt for the grinder as an object was accentuated and sustained by the interrupting barrier of the window, which, in contradiction, allowed certainty that the desired object was available while frustrating any final union with that object, any touch, any gratification of attainment. Desire is sustained through delay and Duchamp's works are conjugations, positions of evasions and exposures. A door that is both open and closed. A highly occult, obscure glossary of dadaist images and procedures that you can quite literally see through. Materials of insistently ordinary availability suspiciously transformed into works of art purely by context and/or slight intervention. A final work in which we glimpse, through a peephole in a wooden door, an elaborate and obscure arrangement of kitsch and puppetry. The glimpse. (De Kooning, the most eroticized of the abstract expressionists, referred to himself as a "slipping glimpser.")

But reading poems that explicitly deal with sex, like Verlaine's rough trade poem "A Thousand and Three," or section 11 of "Song of Myself," ending with its souse of spray, or Archilochos's poem 18, praising "her fine, hard, bared crotch," or Joyce Mansour's "In the Gloom on the Left," which begins, "Why my legs around your neck," I'm struck not so much by a power of evasion to prolong desire or with language's inadequacy to refer so much as its overabundance and adequacy. It refers again and again, producing physiological charge by way of transubstantiation of sign into flesh. It is quibbling to note each representation's inability to convey the whole of sexual desire and experience as a failing of language. If anything, want-more may be an indication of glut, of endless particulars. It is the very overabundance of referential capacity that makes for the breakdown of any single referential stability, or at least conscribes it. As proof we have the countless terms for sexual acts and organs, and once we are in the realm of sexual action, nearly any phrase has a splendid, dirty potential: box with Richard, buff one's helmet, baby in a boat, lion tamer, grotto, gusset, pearl dive, zazzle.

"The pleasure of the text is that moment when my body pursues its own ideas—for my body does not have the same ideas I do." Unlike the rational mind, which seeks to fortress itself as a site of privilege, control, and certainty, writing about sex takes as its subject position a position that is alternative and in flux, be it Coyote in the Native American tales completely buried except for his red "sticking-out thing" or Kenneth Koch's taping the lover to the wall in a paradox of control in "The Art of Love," or the nearly endless arrangements of limbs wedded to a superfluidity of naming in André Breton and Paul Eluard's collaboration from *The Immaculate Conception* called "Love," "6. When the man and the woman lie on their backs, with one of the woman's legs across the man's belly, it is the *broken mirror. . . .* 23.

When the woman bends over on her hands and feet like a quadruped and the man is standing, it is the *earring.*" In Dryden's translation of Lucretius's "The Position," poetic decorum is aptly and periodically fitted to the prescription for "correct" position for intercourse: coupling couplets.

The Romantics, in their early attempts at the creation of psychology, are naturally indirect in their explorations of sexuality. But who can forget that "strenuous tongue / [that] Can burst Joy's grape against his palate fine" near the end of Keats's "Ode on Melancholy"? "Glut thy sorrow" indeed. And in a remarkable attempt of transference, Wordsworth's inclusion in book IX, "Residence in France," of *The Prelude* (and later exclusion of), a completely tangential fable of star-crossed lovers in the very place that, in terms of the autobiography the poem is creating, he should fess up to his involvement with Annette Vallon (we'll return to this). And then there's Coleridge's tale of imagination interruptus, "Kubla Khan," with its exploration of a "deep romantic chasm . . . A savage place!" where a "woman [is] wailing for her demon lover!" "Beware, beware! / His flashing eyes, his floating hair!" Coleridge proposes this inflamed male to be met years later by Plath's female version in "Lady Lazarus": "Beware / Beware /

Out of the ash / I rise with my red hair / And I eat men like air." Hot stuff.

There are problems in writing about sex, of course. Beginning with the matter of pornography and obscenity. In 1973, the U.S. Supreme Court, in *Miller v. California*, determining whether a work is "obscene and therefore unprotected by the first amendment," came up with this three-step test:

1. That the average person, applying contemporary community standards, would find that the work, taken as a whole, appeals to prurient interest and
2. That the work depicts or describes in a patently offensive way, as measured by contemporary community standards, sexual conduct specifically defined by the applicable law and
3. That a reasonable person would find that the work, taken as a whole, lacks serious literary, artistic, political and scientific value.

Where to begin? May I say that in regards to sexual activity, even the thinking of sexual activity, I have yet to meet a reasonable person. Eros is NOT reasonable. Average? Contemporary community standards? I've lived in small midwestern towns and in the Bay Area where

I've detected just a slight difference in community standards. I am not trying to make an argument (I'm NOT
making an argument at all, I'm just trying to be convincing!) in support of child pornography or snuff films
so much as insist upon the necessary wildness and dis-
orienting power of writing about sex. Sex is the ruination
of politics, not the sad discharge of it. Difference is at the
center of sexual energy, not just heterosexual difference,
but the difference of homosexuality, which is the other
other, and even when the difference is not conventionally
manifested as boy on girl (as in Gertrude Stein's "Lifting
Belly"), the play and instabilities of Eros come from a dia-
logic exchange so that at any moment the subject can
become object and the object subject, not insisting upon
the fixity of any one state but upon momentary positions: "Do we see the bird jelly I call it. I call it something
religious" (Stein); "When only one of the legs is extended,
it is past midnight" (Breton and Eluard, taking turns).
Within the charged field of intimacy, how like reading
and writing, there can be no community standards.

> "Let a hundred flowers bloom, let a hundred schools
> of thought contend."
>
> —Mao

"Neither culture nor its destruction is erotic; it is the
seam between them, the fault, the flaw, which becomes

so" (Barthes). We are enticed toward the multiplication of Ovidian positions and seams. Whitman: "Urge and urge and urge, / Always the procreant urge of the world" and word. Disjunct between convention, between cultural imperatives for order and the ripping of the gown, is the site of poetry; it causes trouble, is transgressive, puts its tongue everywhere. "Yes, Coyote said to the unmarried girl, you should be going to the mountain top. When you will see a red thing sticking out that will be a power.... She saw it, she was lifting up her dress, she looked around her, Coyote said to her, You should be masturbating on your power!... Now she was taking in the guardian spirit."

In writing about sex, the word achieves a superadequacy, the power to elide with thing, to have both precedent over it in such a way as to call for the thing it names, and as a way of blending with it. The naming of god as sacramental act that must be partitioned off from any use devoid of doxology allows for no talking dirty. Hence the screen between the worldly confessor and the priest that filters the passage of one use of language to another. The complete union of sign and signified is supposedly the province of god and as such the superadequacy of language when referring to sex dangerously verges on enacting sex and therefore finds itself with the sacred realm of word becoming thing, with carnal rather than spiritual intention, creating a crisis of the allowable. "The text of pleasure is sanctioned by babble." In *Roth v. United States* (1957), Justice Harlan wrote in support of obscenity laws, "The state can reasonably draw inference that over a long period of time the indiscriminate dissemination of materials, the essential character of which is to degrade sex, will have an eroding effect on moral standards." The indiscriminate dissemination of sexually explicit materials is seen as a form of desacrilization, the irony being that the sanctified version of sexual discourse is silence or clinical and mechanical. Just say no when saying makes it so.

The writing of sex is always a perversion, a turning away from silence, of violating the sacred partitions of order and community standards and reasonableness, often to the creation of new communities. Its identity is dependent upon both recognition and revulsion. It's a sad commentary that the argument supporting the explicit photos by Mapplethorpe in the big NEA brouhaha years back was based upon the notion that art and titillation are incommensurate so that critical sophistication sanitized itself by concentrating on composition, on the play of hues and contours at the expense of being affected by a picture of a man putting his fist up another's ass. The primary aesthetic argument in support of the NEA and Mapplethorpe was one of de-

tachment, disconnection, of insisting upon a glacial
remove. But the life-affirming perversity of art and its
attendant optimism in the reformation of identity is
not a result of gaps and delays primarily; it is what is IN
the gap: what is glimpsed is the proving flood of detail,
the gush in the gash, the visual's as well as language's
power to flush the nerves to the point of acquiring
flesh, lubricity. Because of its trespass into the sacred
realm, the poetics of sex will always be in violation. The
glimpses it affords are in a breach of ordered, seamless
appearance, where the word surges into the thing and
the mouth that forms it.

"The thin red jellies within you, or within me."

—Whitman

"What is it that really matters? For the poppy, that
the poppy disclose its red: for the cabbage, that it run
up into weakly fiery flower."

—D. H. Lawrence

A few weeks ago I got into an argument about tobiko.
One of my tablemates remarked that if only we were
smart enough, we could understand the function of this
flying fish roe's florescent orange. Now anyone who has
watched a few nature shows, seen a long curved beak
that perfectly fits the orchid or some plant's extrusion

of sugar to feed the ants that protect it from other insects, can easily, misguidedly think that evolution is a
problem solver, that the individuation of species is pur-
poseful, in short that the color of those eggs must
be performing some necessary task for survival. It may
be but evolution doesn't solve problems, it doesn't react
to environment so much as changes in the environment select some, not all, aspects over others that are
favorable for survival in any given sphere. Evolution
has no intention; rather through random lurches in
mutation, through aleatory variety, it finds fits, makes
do. Mutation is a mistake in copying! I do not believe
in perfection or perfectibility (although the shark sure
comes close). I believe in the simultaneity of a changing environment and changing response to and in that
environment, and those responses becoming part of
the environment. Our world is constantly flickering,
dapple-dawn-drawn, patterns emerge and vanish like
clouds beneath waves. We are momentary. The singular
orange of that sushi is just as likely solely expressive; it
proclaims its existence, doesn't justify it through what
sort of job it does. Purposeless is not meaninglessness.
I wasn't put on this planet to explain myself. The variety of nature is too astonishing to explain as a form of
utility, it's just not necessary. Functional concern does
not look for plethora, it looks for single solutions. God
must have loved beetles, Darwin remarked of their astonishing array. Myriad minded let us be. Why? Maybe

to be loved. "To show the balloon famously" (Stein). As I figure it, however we construe the divine, if we've replaced god with art as Stevens says, it is surely without necessity. Art initiates/irritates us into plenitude, it makes the world and our consciousness more. Art asserts through affect that it is alive, singularly.

But what IS poetry for? The question of utility has bugged poets for quite a while. In Western civilization, the purpose for and of art has been on a long, strange journey to such a degree that one purpose, and sometimes seemingly the only purpose, is for art to turn against itself. When in 1917, Duchamp bought a coat rack on a whim, and, noticing people were tripping over it as it lay on his floor, nailed it there; he trapped the ironies and negations that have thrown such huge shadows on the production of art over the next century. What did he do? He took a prefabricated, manufactured object and removed it from its very purpose; he destroyed its utility. Art became a travesty of context, something you trip over. The authority of the artist is self-parodic, highlighting itself as whim rather than wisdom, conceptual rather than a perfection of technique. The rearticulating of this joke has led us to a crisis of irony: art seems to function solely as a debacle of context, a suspension and suspicion of traditional modes of expertise in favor of appropriation, an endless procession of quote marks, the deconstruction of any imaginative act into a triumph of depthless allusion and arch remove. Art becomes the ruination of utility. Music, painting, poetry, performance becoming a kind of purging tantrum, its use disruptive to its own usefulness, has bequeathed us an unavoidable irony toward the possibility of any art's sincerity; it is the rupture of elsewhere in any sense of belonging. We as poets now face the danger of a fundamental estrangement. While such irony gives us powerful displacements of consciousness, of self-consciousness, it also threatens to orphan us from the primary efficacy and use of our art.

POETRY ATROPHIES WHEN IT STRAYS TOO FAR FROM THE HUMAN PANG

The Artist

(Aztec)

The artist: disciple, abundant, multiple, restless.
The true artist: capable, practicing, skillful;
maintains dialogue with his heart, meets things with
     his mind.
The true artist: draws out all from his heart,
works with delight, makes things calm, with sagacity,
works like a true Toltec, composes his objects, works
     dexterously, invents;
arranges materials, adorns them, makes them adjust.

The carrion artist: works at random, sneers at people,
makes things opaque, brushes across the face of
    things,
works without care, is a thief.

(English version by Denise Levertov)

In, for want of a better word, primitive poems, like those collected in the indispensable anthologies edited by Jerome Rothenberg, we find none of the nagging displacements that threaten to numb our art. Here the artist's fundamental allegiances are to what his/her heart says, what the world is and what the mind adds, and materials do not take precedence over vision and insight but are in dialogue with it. Art is the manifestation of choices in a charged field. Poetry, song, incantation, spell, all have effect in the world; they are there to go between and incarnate our beginnings and our ends. Through primary concerns, primitive art refuses estrangement from the natural world and the divine. In their fabrics we can find intimations of the most innovative poetry of the last century, such as collage and collaboration in African praise poems, surrealist structures and visualizations in spirit journeys. As Rothenberg writes in the preface of *Symposium of the Whole,* "My own choice has been to write from the side of a moderism that sees itself as challenging limits and changing ways of speaking/thinking/doing that have too long

, interesting . . .

robbed us of the freedom to be human to the full extent of our powers and yearnings." Our psychic and physical union with the natural world has never been more imperiled; Christianity in this country insists upon our separation from the animals, orphans us from tigers and ants, absolving us of environmental responsibility. But never has it been more important for us to reconceive identity, heroism, the possibilities of praise, our place in the cosmos both stellar and on the ground. Reality must be called forth; it is not imaginary but it comes into being in collaboration with the imagination. Religion must be improvisational else it be the debasement of the irrational, the coining of the spirit. Death is a mystery to inhabit, maybe "far luckier than we know" (Whitman), what our poetry must animate just as it is animated with a profound blood relation to the natural world.

A Song from *Red Ant Way*

(Navajo)

The red young men under the ground
decorated with red wheels
& decorated with red feathers
   at the center of the cone-shaped house
   I gave them a beautiful red stone—
   when someone does the same for me
   I'll walk the earth
The black young women under the ground

decorated with black wheels
& decorated with black feathers
  at the center of the flat-topped house
  I gave them an abalone shell—
  when someone does the same for me
  I'll walk the earth
From deep under the earth they're starting off
the old men under the earth are starting off
they're decorated with red wheels & starting off
at the center of the cone-shaped house they're
    starting off
because I gave them a beautiful red stone they're
    starting off
when someone does the same for me I'll walk the
    earth like them & starting off
on the red road & on the road they're starting off
The black old women under the earth are starting off
they're decorated with black wheels & starting off
decorated with black feathers & starting off
at the center of the flat-topped house they're
    starting off
because I gave them an abalone shell they're starting off
when someone does the same for me I'll walk the
    earth like them & starting off
from the deep under the earth they're starting off

(translated by Harry Hoijer,
with reworking by Jerome Rothenberg)

It may not be possible for poetry in our time to take on such primary religious, social importance, such integrity. But that doesn't lessen the opportunities for our art. People search for poems when the occasion demands, when emotion requires the ritualized and/or raw powers of poetry. Curse and blessing, disaster and celebration, that is where our poetry is, in the human pang. Discipline is only good for the dispensing of punishment. Art's great obligation is to its own liberty, and by demonstration, the realization of ours. It is not an exercise any more than making love or dying can be practiced. "May it be to the world, what I believe it will be (to some parts sooner, to others later, but finally to all), the signal of arousing men to burst the chains under which monkish ignorance and superstition had persuaded them to bind themselves, and to assume the blessings and security of self-government. . . . All eyes are opened, or opening, to the rights of man. The general spread of the light of science has already laid open to every view the palpable truth, that the mass of mankind has not been born with saddles on their backs, nor a favored few, booted and spurred, ready to ride them legitimately, by the grace of God. These are grounds of hope for others; for ourselves" (Thomas Jefferson).

The writing and reading of poetry are done in a vast number of conditions, with a vast number of aims and social/personal intentions. Any statement about poetry that doesn't acknowledge that in some way must be considered with suspicion. While I hope to keep in mind the heterodoxy of poetic practice, I am nonetheless going to do my best to articulate my thought, which requires to some extent various polarizations. I value intensity but I also value contradiction. Poetic practice has changed throughout time to the increase of the riches of poetry in general, by poets doing what they have been told not to or sensed were discouraged/disallowed from doing. At the center of any artistic practice is a resistance as well as a contrary impulse to identify, to stand off from the tribe and to be part of it. Poetry is an assertive force. Even though the superlative Marianne Moore says in her *Paris Review* interview that her poems are poems because no one knows what else they could be, I find this notion of a poem being a poem by default, by its being too weird, its syntax too fucked-up or whatever for it to be any other kind of writing, a lazy notion at best. Every poem must assert itself as poetry actively. Poetry, like any art form, is recognized through its relationship to precedents/convention. While all art forms evolve to some extent through resistance to convention, that resistance is defined by the set of conventions it resists and with which it remains in identification. If that resistance presupposes itself as resisting all conventions, at most it can accomplish oddity, muddy water, obscurity, unrecognizability, all of which may be important aspects of poetry but they do not in themselves make a poem. A poem asserts itself as poetry by being in dialogue with what it resists; therefore those resistances need to be composed, focused, limited. Form never manifests itself as unlimited. (Who wants to read a poem that doesn't end?) To assume complete originality, the complete independence from convention (the past, limits) is wildly self-involved, megalomaniacal, foolish, perhaps repugnant. Originality is not the denial of origins, it is both the acknowledgment of them, the acquiescence and exploration of that trace of history, the common imperative, while being in cantankerous, maybe competitive objection and declaration otherwise.

People use language for two reasons: to be understood and not to be understood.

The first goal aspires toward a perfect lucidity, the transparence of a universal idiom, the ability to refer uncluttered by any peculiarity of referent, any impurity, all mitigation disappeared. The second arises either from within an utterly private, expressive state or is constituted as the free play of impenetrable code. Either eruptive interiority or ultimate detachment, this language is not dependent upon reception except perhaps in the most intimate of terms. The first goal yearns for community and seeks to preserve it through recognized, accepted, and repeated decorums. The second transcribes the impossible terms of intimacy, resides in strangeness, its signs opaque in that they refer not so much to the outside world as to an inner origin of utterance or to themselves in a play of disconnection and discord. The first goal describes, attributes, addresses, devotes. The second startles, baffles, originates, its beguilements are a physical presence undeferred, it makes material of its release, its words present in the first order.

How do we understand each other when we say I love you?

To simplify, this is a distinction between a communicative state and an expressive state. There's the fire: we must leave the building versus Yikes! Poetry is in perpetual negotiation between these two urges. Between interior and exterior, between liberty and obligation, anarchy and order, self and community, referent and what it can refer to, sign and thing. Between defamiliarized and recognizable rhetorics. Between Scylla and Charybdis. There is no avoiding casualties, there will be losses to the whirlpool that pulls everything into itself and to the monster that destroys through centrifugal sprawl. These are the two forces that form must come to terms with. The imaginative tendency to include everything, through disjunction and wildness, allows all to enter a poem, versus the concentrating gravities of formal control, of will and limits. We must work to lose control when control has become too limiting, just as we must assert more vigorously the presence of choice to counter a too great loss of control. The making of poems is in constant tack between these two poles and there will always be poems that fail in this zigzag sail.

As an art of words, poetry depends on making these words appear materialized. SOME THINGS MUST BE MADE OPAQUE TO BE SEEN. The medium appears through the accentuation of itself as mitigating factor (this would be better if I didn't understand it) and as sound or design. This accentuation must befuddle assumptions of community almost successfully, make a shambles of the habituation of expectation. "Surprise is the greatest source of what is new," writes Guillaume Apollinaire in his proclamation "The New Spirit and the Poets." "The richest domain being the imagination, the least known, whose extent is infinite, it is not astonishing that the name of poet has been particularly reserved for those who look for the new joys which mark out the enormous spaces of the imagination." We know the message is delivered by a god when the god's radiance obscures the import of the message. This accounts in part for poetry's necessary difficulty. We expect language to deliver information purposefully, but in poetry those means of delivery are impeded. The words of a poem always want us to notice their appearance and manner as much as the news they deliver. Poetry is not efficient. If you want to learn how to cook a lobster, it's probably best not to look to poetry. But if you want to see the word *lobster* in all its reactant oddity, its pied beauty, as if for the first time, go to poetry. And if you want to know what it's like to be that lobster in the pot, that's in poetry too.

> "Of course it is wonderfully beautiful, only when it is still a thing irritating annoying stimulating then all quality of beauty is denied to it."
>
> —Stein

When I lived at the Fine Arts Work Center in Provincetown years ago, I got to know the sculptor and painter Charles Spurrier. Walking into his studio was like going into a bombed cathedral. Full of glorious debris and hazard, surely there was some primitive, devotional work being done here. I had the sense too that the reckless god worshipped and housed there required this destruction. Extension cords snaked the floor through stacks of railroad ties, piles of glass, buckets of paint, beach stones, fishnets, sheet metals rusted and new.

And the tools! Somewhere in all this, in a shower of sander sparks, would be Charles, looking part cherub, part ax murderer. His work was cataclysmic, patched together, slashed apart, set on fire. A piece was more temporarily abandoned than finished for the formality of a show, and if it wasn't bought, it went back into the system, quite possibly to be sawed, painted over, or melted down from some more current work. Mostly I was aware of momentary stays against miraculous and horrible metamorphosis. Cocoons cut open. The materials seemed to have a life of their own, took part in both their own creation and destruction simultaneously; the wood of a ladder verged on tearing itself apart to become tree again, metals seemed to be trying to bend and unbend themselves. I had seen him on more than one occasion take a piece and do things to it that, if I didn't know it was his own work, I would have sworn he was committing vandalism. In fact, desecration was part of his process. John Ashbery writes in "The Invisible Avant-Garde," "Most reckless things are beautiful in some way, and recklessness is what makes experimental art beautiful, just as religions are beautiful because of the strong possibility that they are founded on nothing." The Charybdis of devotion and the Scylla of doubt. The risk in Charles's work was that it flirted with, even embraced, forces and attitudes toward materials that to some extent eradicated the art itself, yet this contradiction did not lead to canceling out.

I've always envied visual artists for an obvious, constantly available opportunity to interact with the medium in a primal, physical way. Paint is always ready to be paint, thrown, slathered, sprayed, blotted up. Even in the most elementary energetic exchange, something is always created. Drop cloths are always beautiful. In fact, it is impossible NOT to make something with materials even if the act of using those materials is contrary to intended, conventional usage, even if it resides in refusal. Any act, even one that seems antithetical to our notions of art production, still winds up with something. From there on it is a complex social, economic, personal matter as to whether that something is SOMETHING. To some extent, the history of visual art moves in two directions. The more obvious is the use of materials to create illusion, mimesis: to paint in a way to make us forget we are looking at pigment and glue, make us see the savior's garment, a surface that tricks us into depth. I thought you said death—not depth—perception. In general these tricks of illusion are the basis of our notion of mastery: the better the artist, the better his or her mastery over materials to create illusion. Mastery is always OVER something. The other direction involves the refusal of illusion and the refusal of that sort of dominating expertise. It seeks to offer up paint as paint, a surface as a field of struggle, experimental over design, discovery over certainty of destination. The art becomes a record of process. Mimetic art tends to make its process disappear, whereas this type of art makes us aware of the path of creation, destroying the instantaneous effect of illusion. To divide artists and works squarely into stables of concern is, of course, a rather dumb thing to do, but what I'd like to suggest is that power can come from these opposing attitudes and practices coming into contact in single works. As Vivaldi said, the struggle is between innovation and harmony. It's always one thing AND the other. "The innumerable compositions and decompositions," writes Keats in a letter. "More wreck and less discourse," writes Hopkins, thinking of writing/righting his "Deutschland." Many great works of illusion contain aspects of the primacy of materials just as those that seem entirely taken up with process still throw representational shadows. Michelangelo's David impresses us not just as a lifelike giant but also for its stoniness, just as Jackson Pollock's *Number 8, 1949* may strike us as a vision of a firing neural network as well as a catastrophe of paint.

But certainly the twentieth century has seen great emphasis put on materials used in process over mimesis, over representation and illusion. Impressionism is more than painting not what the eye sees but how it sees, as Degas said; it is also painting what the paintbrush can do. It is a good place to see one tradition giving way to what will become another. Indeed, some of Monet's haystacks strike me most as dispersal of form for the sake of color, of, finally, paint. One outer limit of giving the supremacy to materials is reached with monochromes: painting entirely one color more or less evenly applied. To come upon a surface entirely black or white or red in a museum is like arriving at silence at the end of symphonic busyness. It seems to be the point that painting has moved toward but been previously afraid to reach, painting's universal language, saying everything in a first word. Gut-wrenchingly refreshing, outlandish, audacious. The end of crucifixions and coronations and troop movements and anatomy lessons: a calm, a kind of death. (But of course off to the side, there's a Warhol soup can, another coronation, or is it another crucifixion?) The fact that one particular work or one particular artist need not be singled out for appreciation indicates a kind of obliteration of what we normally think of as mastery, substituting artistic near-anonymity. The hand of the individual too has vanished. The clichéd response, and from my limited survey the most common, is that these works, and other more gestural abstract works, could be done by anyone or a child. That this is used as a pejorative implies more about who is saying it than the art itself: for that critic art must be beyond inherent human capabilities; the artist must be an individual far from birth, closer to death, the activity of making art only possible after years and years of discipline, of denial, failure, far from first marks and realization.

One of the devilish sources of innovation in art has always been doing something that everyone thinks cannot and/or should not be done. One of the primary intentions in the making of art is to fly in the face of the acceptable. That intention is what I sense brought entirely to the surface in monochromes, part of a quintessentially modern aesthetic, how the effectiveness, the legitimacy of a work of art resides not just in what it is but also in what it refuses or denies, what it is not, a kind of negative presence, what Jurij Lotman calls in *The Structure of the Artistic Text* "a minus-device." We appreciate X for what it is not as much as for what it is. Not a trick, not yet another elaborate advertisement. Instead a primary reduction: paint on a surface, material. And in many ways, this reduction is a violation, a desecration. It is what isn't allowed.

Compared to what I was doing in my studio, Charles's work seemed far more powerful. Imagine a poem that retained the raw energy of materials, of language itself.

Charles would wage his wars, labor to break his work out of its thick shell, occasionally being struck by a mystic imperative to go to the dump or the beach in search of new materials. What tame, memory-dependent work I was doing. How polite my poems were, how still they sat, how representational. We poets talked about craft, but what we meant were tricks and illusions. THE WRITING OF POETRY IS NOT A CRAFT.

WE ARE MAKING BIRDS, NOT BIRDCAGES. We might as well have been discussing how to hold your pinkie finger while drinking tea. Poetry as the manipulation of craft elements: give me a break, a smashing, at least a little rattle! I began to wonder if a way beyond this conventional staleness, these poems about how sad and terrible things happened to us, poems in which we describe a field only to realize at the end, dismal epiphany, that Mommy never cometh again, wonder if a way out of such earnest fakery could be in discovering a physicality in and of language. Words, however, are very different materials than paint and rock. In fact, it's a stretch to call them material at all. "You can't say things," writes Michael Palmer. Still, when one of my students a few years back turned in fifteen blank crumpled sheets of paper called "Writer's Block" to an undergraduate poetry class, I had to give her mildly appreciative marks. (I don't believe in writer's block,

writing well is very easy; it's writing horribly, the horrible work necessary to do to get to writing well, that
is so difficult one may just not be willing to do it.) Sure
it was too easy, infinitely copyable, conceptual rather
than very actualized, even "unauthored," but wasn't
it, in itself, a valid critique of poetry and its identity-
mongering? "I fall upon the thorns of life! I bleed!"
Don't valid critiques of art, the opposite of revolu-
tions that tend toward orthodoxy, tend to become art
themselves? Aren't our cherished notions of originality,
of the willed singularity of a line of poetry, a kind of
nervous reaction to the wild democracy of language?
(I always tell my students not to worry about originality; just try to copy the manners and musics of the
various, the more various the better, poetries you love:
your originality will come from your inability to copy
well: YOUR GENIUS IS YOUR ERROR.) Perhaps, just
as our social intentions seek to force the world into a
single image, many of our artistic intentions limit possibility, restrict the imagination. Perhaps the drive to
represent itself is a form of oppression, a fist of fear and
power, and what we should be doing is EXPRESSING.
If that is true, then isn't desecration itself—a freeing of
the materials of art from intention, from ownership,
from illusion, from acceptance—a legitimate artistic
exploration? If that is true, then a poem that isn't written makes some sense. Maybe to some extent, all art is

already desecration, not just Andy Warhol's silk screening of JFK with his head blown open across Jackie's lap, robbing by reproduction a public event of its sacredness and turning it into decoration, mass media; perhaps even Botticelli's *Annunciation* has desecrated our imaginings of god's workings, has destroyed an angel by giving it fixed appearance.

"toward" begins Sapphic fragment number 127. What is moving toward what, we do not know, but the cut-off preposition conveys an urgency even in its inspecificity, an urgency of relation in peril. It is a possibility, drenched in suggestion, incomplete, a shimmer, not a nail. The poem, its remains, halts and starts like a voice racked with sobs and silences, a voice wiped out by interference. "love, I say, will become strong" is the most grammatically and thematically complete phrase in Guy Davenport's translation of the poem, but it is both undercut by the previous "no longer than to the day after tomorrow to be loved" and the perforation of the poem, the tears: love may become strong but it won't last long, won't be able to survive the passage of time whole, unmarked, or unshattered. The document of the poem, the condition of the text, the papyrus remains that may have been gathered, as so many of our Greek fragments were, from the wrappings of mummies, testifies beyond the poem's assertions of content. This irony, this evident contradiction of the power of love, enhances the poem's heroic sentiment. Love, and poetry, are as much subject to ruin as anything on this earth. "of the arrows" ends what we have of the poem, and we can only guess at what ways this phrase fits into the development of the original poem. Was it part metaphor or indeed direct reference to ruin, violence, and death? It, like so much of the poem, is cloaked (choked) in silence. Each phrase comes from a voice struggling to exist. While it proclaims itself, it also evidences its very repudiation. "That is how the past exists," writes Hugh Kenner in *The Pound Era*, "phantasmagoric weskits, stray words, random things recorded. The imagination augments, metabolizes, feeding on all it has to feed on, such scraps." Our reading of this fragment is enhanced by its deterioration, by its destruction. The utterance of the poem is made powerful by the gaps surrounding it; it is moving in part due to its inconsistencies, opacities, aporia, incompletion. The poem is ripped to shreds and we cannot read it without experiencing that ripping, without being made aware of the poem's and, by extension, the poet's fragility. The fragment becomes a just, evocative embodiment of both the passionate inner life of an individual, those violences and needs, as well as the larger violences brought about by history, its neglect and terrible forays. Again Barthes in *The Pleasure of the Text:* "It is this flash itself which seduces, or rather: the staging of an appearance-as-disappearance. . . . it is not violence which affects pleasure, nor is it destruction which interests it; what pleasure wants is the site of a loss, the seam, the cut, the deflation, the *dissolve* which seizes the subject in the midst of bliss." Perhaps Orpheus turned around SO he could see Eurydice vanish, so that his desire would be endless and endless source to song. The moment of appearance bracketed and penetrated by annihilation. *is poetry.*

The use of fragment in contemporary work has become far too subsumed under yet another mode of convention: postmodern sentimentality which assumes that language, like culture and being, is always already broken. It's one thing for Paul Celan to reduce his work to fragmentation through the pressures the use of German brings about for a German Jew; it is a far different thing when someone suggests in a workshop that a poet try revising her poem into fragments. THERE IS NOTHING WRONG WITH OUR LANGUAGE. Children know that. The fragment used in this way exhibits nothing more than a failure to complete a sentence, be it through laziness or inability to compose musically; it does nothing whereas the Sapphic fragment includes more than itself: it includes its own absence, its own nonbeing. Simultaneously we are aware of the power of words to simulate and evoke feeling, and the fact that words are only words, stain on a surface susceptible to erasure, tear, fire, loss. A presence simultaneously created and destroyed, inseparable from its own desecration. Powerfully X and its denial at once. Like that moment in *The Wizard of Oz,* my favorite, when Toto pulls back the Wizard's curtain and the small guy running the thing shouts into his pyrotechnics, "Pay no attention to that man behind the curtain." We are aware of power and vulnerability simultaneously, a whorl of masking and unmasking, presence and illusion; we are tacking, tacking, double-minded.

Some things, like sewer pipes, we want to go only in one direction. But art that is at odds with itself, its own being, that contains seeds, signs, slashes of its own demise, embodies the conflicts of what it is to be alive. To be both here and not here, flesh and mind, physical and metaphysical, mortal yet unable to conceive of one's own death. "The staging of an appearance-as-disappearance." "O, for a Life of Sensations," writes Keats. "Ode to a Nightingale" also confronts and is confronted by the boundaries of its own being. When Barthes writes, "A 'living contradiction': a split subject, who simultaneously enjoys, through the text, the consistency of his selfhood and its collapse, its fall," he might have been describing Keats and the movement of this ode from intensity to intensity, one canceling the other out, only to end in a primal and surrealist confusion between what is real and what is dream, a collapse into a list of prepositional phrases: "Past . . . over . . . up . . . In . . ." The poem suggests that existence itself, its whole, is a blur, and we can only be aware of momentary vividness, of meaning as moment and its undoing. "So that meaning can begin and doing so be undone" (Ashbery). As soon as any moment of insight and position is extended into a more systematic vision, it falters, crumbles. "To thy high requiem become a sod." From the outset, the speaker is in a tangle of desire and repulsion, living and dying, feeling and unfeeling: how on earth can a "numbness pain"? Well, it does, just as the poem's overall arc conveys implicit contradiction. Throughout, the exuberance of the bird both calls the poet out of his deathlike and death-liking lethargy and leads him back toward it. The world of sensation, of living, is fraught with its opposite. "Where youth grows pale, and specter-thin, and dies; / Where but to think is to be full of sorrow," yet it is also the fecund world the poet celebrates: "The coming musk-rose, full of dewy wine, / The murmurous haunt of flies on summer eves." Critics who have pointed to the former lines as some of Keats's weakest writing have entirely missed the point that the reduction in musicality toward a language closer to plain speech parallels the thematic modulation of the poem. As the poet hungers for escape, each escape leads to the very thing he wishes to evade, which in turn leads to an exhausted revelation about the self as a presence both materializing and vanishing. "I have been half in love with easeful Death" is a statement of identity based upon the end of identity, its negation. While on one hand, the poet can never escape the self, the poem demonstrates that the self is not a fixed thing, rather a movement: a collection of arrived-at and abandoned impulses and conflicting conclusions, one X over another. Throughout, the poet listens to his language as much as to the bird, and the poem becomes about itself, its own tracings and dismantlings and flares of desire and repudiation until, in the last stanza, the poet is only aware of what is illusive: the bird moves toward its own silencing, its unbeing. Yet the bird vanished is still the bird just as the self dismantled is the self.

The poem then is a record of its own unsettling, a trace of the mind's unsatisfied and unsatisfiable search for resolution, for escape, to know itself through self-creation and to unknow itself. Poetry itself can lead only to "verdurous gloom and winding mossy ways"; in all the brilliances of lyric invention, we "cannot see what flowers are at [our] feet." This movement exemplifies what Terry Eagleton, in *Literary Theory,* calls "an unsettling venture into the inner void of the text which lays bare the illusoriness of meaning, the impossibility of truth and the deceitful guiles of all discourse." For Keats, the poet is the self as the poem creates that self to record it, the poem is where the poet chases after that self only to enact a cycle of discovery (creation) and uncertainty (destruction). "Every mental pursuit takes its reality and worth from the ardour of the pursuer," Keats writes in a letter. The process of pursuit rather than any final outcome is what "Ode to a Nightingale" enacts, an inability to find an illusion or solution that will not be marked over, x-ed out. It takes its being as much from denial as assertion.

What the Sappho fragment and Keats's ode share is a content that arises as much from process as from subject, and that process disrupts the poem, its consistency and coherence. For Sappho, the process is much more violent, and comes from outside her intention—she wasn't aiming to write fragments; it must be said that part of the power of her work is in spite of its being in fragments. But both poems are enlarged beyond their own making by an included unmaking; they exhibit contradiction in their very existence to the reader. They are both composed of swift assertive (re)marks, bold intentions within a field of opposite pressures toward silence, opacity, holes, tears, slashes, erasures. The poems are made and unmade, minus-devices of themselves. With Keats, we begin to see that even the intensity of self-conscious making, apart from physical forces, can disrupt the poem, move it toward demonstration of its own (in)capacities and contradictions so that it begins to blur, rip, deny itself.

Next slide: in Matisse's *Portrait of Olga Merson,* two heavy black strokes violate the suggested representationalism of the portrait. Their boldness suggests both anger and revision: they seem quick, lashed out, although their parallel contours conversely suggest a more willed, careful, and deliberate impulse. While they both destroy the illusion of realism, they also partake of the shape of the subject's body: the larger line on the left, after cutting the breast, joins the outline of the hip for a moment, helps nestle the forearm undisturbed before plunging across the lap like a sword. These lines have the same weight as some of the general outlines of the form, which also gives them their special significance: that is, they both partake of the illusion and destroy it. While much in the painting arises from what is outside it, arises from the features of Olga Merson, those two lines also come from the pressures of composition, as composition of shape, color, stroke. Yet they influence the illusion: Merson's face has shifted, her head turned, flinching perhaps, to align herself with one of the strokes so it doesn't skewer her chin, doesn't obliterate her face. The original position of her head is still apparent as smudge, like movement in a slow-shuttered photograph. What gives the portrait power is this tension between mimesis (the image of Olga Merson) and the material (paint, the brush strokes). One says: Out there; the other says: Here. This tension suggests that the material has a life as present as the subject's—it can cause her to move. It is as if we see a caught moment in the struggle between the exterior world and the interior, the imagination, each tearing at the other: the model's calm, somewhat suffering expression under siege from the black slashes carries a sense of the vulnerability of physical form. Soon, the black lines will have their obliterating way, destroying not only Olga Merson but also the painting itself.

Part of the mission of art, especially since the avant-garde of the late nineteenth and twentieth centuries, has been to break from what the dadaist Richard Huelsenbeck called "the motives of the bourgeois . . . there were artists and bourgeois. You had to love one and hate the other." Because "the soul is by nature volcanic," any artist's creation that did not capture the "spontaneous eruption of possibilities" was merely repackaging of bourgeois, accepted, stale sensibility, "an endless lullaby." The imitation of nature was itself a lie because it upheld established preconceptions, preserved power structures, and repressive philosophies that both bored and sent men to slaughter in the trenches of World

War I. Dada, along with Futurism, was the first of a series of vanguards that culminated in Surrealism, each making rupture, surprise, hoax, humor, violence, outrage goals of art, in creation and response—in short, cultivating all that was not acceptable as art. A break from the past had to be incited, which meant a break with the past's uses of artistic materials. "Dada wanted to frighten mankind out of its pitiful impotence," declared Hans Arp. And part of what was so revitalizing, so shocking and disruptive, was the desecration of art itself, of both the sacred production and the sacred materials.

"If I shout:
Ideal, Ideal, Ideal,
Knowledge, Knowledge, Knowledge,
Boomboom, Boomboom, Boomboom,
I have given a pretty faithful version of progress, law, morality, and all other fine qualities that various highly intelligent men have discussed in so many books," blasted Tristan Tzara in one of his umpteen dada manifestos. In fact, the manifesto itself became a kind of anti-art form: art that refused to be art and was about itself. "no more masterpieces," shouted Tzara. "NO MORE LOOKS! / NO MORE WORDS!" with a footnoted "No more manifestos." Our business is booming! The incendiary salvos launched against the complacency in art,

in the public, in the conception of self, a kind of anti-everything bomb, culminated in this recipe:

> Take a newspaper.
> Take some scissors.
> Choose from this paper an article of the length you
>   want to make your poem.
> Cut out the article
> Next carefully cut out each of the words that makes
>   up this article and put them all in a bag.
> Shake gently.
> Next take out each cutting one after the other.
> Copy conscientiously in the order in which they left
>   the bag.
> The poem will resemble you.
> And there you are—an infinitely original author of
>   charming sensibility, even though unappreciated
>   by the vulgar herd.

I don't know of anything else that so thoroughly lampoons, undercuts, and explodes so many of our vaulted, spoken, and unspoken pieties about authorial control, about authority. Aside from jabbing at the romantic notion of the poet, godlike, standing in the center of the transcendent vision of his work (his or her doesn't seem right here, does it?), "the true and only doctor; he knows

and tells; he is the only teller of news; for he was present and privy to the appearance which he describes" as
Emerson put it, well, bomb that poet, that malpractice.
We move from Shelley's beautiful notion that poets are
the unknown legislators of the world through Rimbaud's
that poets are the legislators of the unknown to dada's
poets are fuckheads just like everyone is a fuckhead.
Aside from detonating our cherished notions of originality and mastery, what interests me most here is that
the assault on poetry in general is based upon handling language not as sign, but as thing. And something
handled in a way in which it wasn't intended or should
be is desecration. Doesn't graffiti desecrate a wall by
making it a surface of expression or obstructing the
pure sacrament of advertisement? Desecration makes
visible what is intended to be invisible, marks over what
is intended to be the final mark or blankness. Tagged
monuments, Mona Lisa with a mustache. What Tzara
lets loose here is a use of language beyond and subver-
sive of accepted referentiality, a way to cut words free
from journals, liberate sounds from the deadening grit
of newspaper, free language from utility, from information. It's better if we don't understand it. Boom.

Words then take on a nearly mystic physicality, a transubstantiation where language is caught in that moment
between being emptied of old usage like a chamber pot

and ready to be charged with new (mis)use. Now this is the craft of poetry: explicit directions for the use of specific materials for a specific outcome. Absurd, of course: simultaneously ascribing to how-to platitudes while pointing toward the outrageous eventuality of such an activity, an activity that sounds an awful lot like the typical creative writing exercise. Dada always has it both ways, and sneers both ways. Here is an aesthetic assertion of uselessness; language is torn from its most stable position as unbiased reportage, disrupted from the production of information and restored (desecrated) to poetry through willful derangement and the consecration of chance. As with Duchamp's *Trap*, which suggests that the highest accomplishment of art is to make us trip over something in the wrong place, something misused, and Meret Oppenheim's mink cup and saucer, which violates the use of the cup with the mink to a destabilizing erotic effect, the point is that art is at odds with utility, it is meant to disrupt the habituations of use. Also at work in Tzara's directive is a fundamental assault on the notion of the coherent self at the center of a work of art and the assumption that that self precedes expression. The self na na na na is an accidental construction from debased materials like everything else, collaged from the wreckage of context, available to us only through sabotage and hoax. The fetishized individuality of the great work of art and the master artist is reduced to schoolboy cutting, aleatory whim, and perhaps most deliciously, copying conscientiously. The self is plagiarized.

LET US GET BETTER AT NOT KNOWING WHAT WE'RE DOING

When Ezra Pound in "Hugh Selwyn Mauberley" writes, "His true Penelope was Flaubert," he was subscribing to an alternative to what he called slither and wobble in the writing of his immediate predecessors. Espousing Flaubert's notorious concentration on compression, stylistic refinement, and the long, difficult labor of writing and yielding a concomitantly rather abstemious output, Pound sets forth as an ultimate ideal "le mot juste," the right word, the exact word. In his chatty dictum "A Few Don'ts by an Imagiste," Pound commands: "Use no superfluous word, no adjective which does not reveal something. . . . Use either no ornament or good ornament." But beneath what seems to be sensible advice lurks a profound denial, a denial of the possible exploratory powers of language that is not utterly subsumed by known, preexistent intention, leading to the crystalline accomplishments of imagism but also to its austerities and emotive limitations; compression becomes confused with dessication. "I have sketched, botched, slogged, groped," writes Flaubert midway through *Madame Bovary* in March 1852. "Per-

haps I'm on the right track now. Oh, what a rascally
thing is style. I don't believe you have any idea what kind
of book this one is. I'm trying to be as buttoned-up in it
as I was unbuttoned in the others and to follow a geo-
metrically straight line. No lyricism, no reflection, the
personality of the author absent. It won't be fun to read."
Sure doesn't seem like it was fun to write either.

But IT'S OKAY TO ENJOY WRITING! Poetry need not
be a distillation of suffering! "I sometimes wonder why
my arm doesn't fall off my body from weariness and why
my head doesn't dissolve into mush. I lead a harsh life
devoid of all external joy . . . for I am often hours chasing
a word and I have more yet to track down," he laments
in the following April. As with Rimbaud, the qualities of
agony and failure are forefront in the process of creation,
but unlike the hallucinatory rewards of glimpsing the unknown that Rimbaud champions, Flaubert's wrecks are
upon the rocks of unachieved certainty. Clarification
and refinement rather than abandonment, the haunting sense of a single, right word out there that must be
hunted down versus a sense of infinite disclosure and
revelation in the possibilities of an exfoliation of language
free from correctness, at liberty. No lyricism, no author
(foreshadowing Eliot's clinical "extinction of personality"), no joy, only the perpetual sense of falling short.
"I have certainly seen the goal recede before me."

"Serious people have a slight odor of carrion."

—Picabia

"If we have no harbor in mind, then no wind seems favorable."

—Coleridge

Anti-corollary: if we have enough wind in mind,
every harbor is favorable.

Hello, Gertrude Stein! Thank you for *Tender Buttons*. It makes me laugh. It is okay to be goofy, it is okay to be funny. Tears are good but they are always archival, they pull us back and down, they mourn, they seek to repeat, but laughter throws us forward, levity raises us, the body opens. Laughter is always unruly. The goofy is the body's blooming in the mind. Let us laugh so hard we disrupt the tragedy! It's hard to think when we laugh and that is one reason, once it was invented, we could not live without it. It is a way of sleeping while feeling intensely awake. The body is jostling itself into rejuvenation. It's like having sex! You're not supposed to do it in court or church or the funeral parlor, which makes them, of course, the funniest of places. To be silly is to be bad in kindergarten, is to wear nothing but a thong under the graduation gown, is to glimpse a fundamental truth about the affairs of mankind and our sad term on earth and be consoled. Freud said one of the reasons we laugh at jokes is because we need to experience again and again hiding and finding. Our love of being fooled is a vital need to recover first recognitions, to make if only for a moment our recognition innocent. For a moment, I think, when we encounter radiant silliness, profound goofiness, we feel double-minded, we stand beside ourselves, fully outside the world of convention that the funny is always foil to, to be fully in some zero-gravity realm of possibility that can only be called pleasure. We laugh not only at the fantastical but also at the truth that is shown to us out of place, devoid of decorum, in disjuncture from our expectations of etiquette, of consistency. To laugh always takes us to the site of rupture, it may be how our body is attempting to educate our consciousness of the moment of its death. Laughter is always brief in its triumph over pain, but in its intensity it suggests too that pain is brief.

They slapped us because we were laughing while people were doing terrible things to each other, atrocities, so they slapped us because we were singing.

"Diamonds in the in the sky."

—Stein

Instead of a discourse that delivers over time a clearer and more finalized representation, a finished-off substitution for its subject, *Tender Buttons* "shows the choice," establishes a system of signs based as much on play, on keep-away and hide-and-seek as static perfection. THE PLAY IS NOT FOR THE GOAL, THE GOAL IS TO PLAY. What begins as definition quickly becomes riddle so that meaning is not based on fixed logical equations but on a constantly shifting web of differences. "A carafe, that is a blind glass" makes fleeting sense, sense by glimpses: a carafe is blind when it can't be seen through (in an object-subject switcheroo); that is, when it is full of red wine. Its usefulness, the carafe's, is at odds with utility—glass is to be seen through. But the carafe will no longer be blind when we have drained the contents, becoming perhaps blind (drunk) ourselves. Instead of organized movements toward a delineated, singular subject within a singular, frozen perspective: a multiplicity demonstrative of chaotic, faceted aspects in the perceiving and writing of the world. Hic. "Act so there is no center," embrace wobble. "Do I wake or dream?" Refute the singular vanishing point that insists all goes into the same oblivion and is defined, shaped by that ultimate oblivion. Instead, *Tender Buttons* destabilizes persistent syntactic arrangements and lexical rigor mortises to assert that "certainly glittering is handsome and convincing," glittering a radiant process of flux and variance. "Is there pleasure when there is a passage, there is when every room is open."

THE PAW PRINT OF THE HOAX CROSSES EVEN THE PUREST SNOW OF OUR ARTISTIC INTENTIONS

How to Replace the Bulb

1. Disconnect the force for 5 minutes at least until bulb is uncaring enough.
2. Take out steel ring by any sharp of tool at place of two gap then leave the glass shield.
3. Put the bulb out of the socket and intersect a young bulb.
4. Intersect the glass shield into the reflector then steel ring under the glass shield.

In the honest-to-god directions above, copied from an insert in the box of a lamp that never quite worked, are the joys of the incorrect word, of misuse. The language in its conventional failure is poetic. LE MOT FAUX. Such "inaccuracies," be they through mistranslation or ineptitude, playfully disorganize our expectation and, in this sabotage of utility, approach art. LE MOT FOU. Words can be given long leashes, there is great possibility in such liberty. Who doesn't love seeing where some wags have rearranged the letters of the carwash/ gas station's sign from "Free with fill-up" to "Feel hr up"? This sort of play, what the situationists called detours, undermines authority with laughter, deranges the claims of advertising to monkey business. It opens itself to the glimpsing of mortal messages that are not exempt from the anarchy of life. Instead of the ideal, we have the body. I thought you said death—not depth-perception—and I love you more for it. In "Preface to a Modern Mythology" in 1926, Louis Aragon states that "Certainty is not reality," arguing that every certainty bases itself upon the error of some previous certainty. All we know for sure is this steady progression of errors so that we "elaborate a changing and always evident truth" yet ask ourselves "why it never seems to satisfy." Error, however, "with its unknown characteristics . . . demands that a person contemplate it for its own sake before rewarding him with the evidence about fugitive reality that it alone could give." There is always eros in errors.

It's Poem English School Time

School rest time over and over again look for you
simply appear and simply disappear
that moment smile face and gently think was
as prince appear and as prince disappear

that moment glad and sad think was
and over and over again once more show me
    simple face

Everybody make noise school is meeting and
    parting place
but anyone anybody don't regret so.
because All men have be different

school happy time also certain.
school uninteresting time also certain.
so was know love.
I is anybody love?
so I want. to love to love.
love time sometimes is stop.

school time   one after another pass even if speak.
that one day new love find.
school time. only one self look hard.
and then sometimes. time is stop.
school time love time is stop.
leave that day is love don't be.
find my love time.

school time one after another pass even if speak.
school time only one self look hard.
school time love time is stop.

school time is too poor.
school time is too sob.
school time certainly is stop.

don't forget this language.

—Kiyoe

My friend James Shea sent me this poem written by one of his students in Japan. The grammatical awkwardness, the lexical wobble, the incompletions and aporia, all convey an unmistakable emotive immediacy. There is work being done here but it conveys liberty through its very errors. What logically is the breakdown of proficiency, of know-how, is productive of an elegant elegiac freshness. The first-mindedness of this poet with this language is indeed something that should not be forgotten. Our language is always a second language and its expressivity resides not just in our proficiency with it but in our playful struggle and ineptitude. Our mistakes are truthful; their music need not be overruled; they may lead us to the unruliness of new freedom.

"The flowers came out, and they were on our side."

—Kenneth Koch

To come upon Amiri Baraka's "It's Nation Time" in *The Norton Anthology of Poetry* (sadly expunged after the third edition), was like finding Grace Slick at Trisha Nixon's wedding trying to electrocute the punch with LSD. Volatile, revolutionary, offensive, certainly dangerous. "It's Nation Time" is a call to black power, a call to riot. The poem begins rather calmly, calling for black identity and cohesiveness: "Time to get / together / time to be one strong fast black energy space." From the outset, through lack of punctuation and emphatic line breaks often breaking through words, it presents itself as a score to be spoken. Sung. Shouted finally. "Time to get up and / be / come / be / come . . ." About halfway through, language itself begins to show signs of stress under an increasingly violent emotion. "Boom / Boom / BOOM." I can't help but feel not only that the poem is demanding to be heard, performed, and by extension, acted out, it is also blowing up *The Norton Anthology.* Shall I compare thee BOOM. While I wandered lonely as BOOM. "Dadadadad." Just typing that line gives a percussive thrill of physicality, of immediacy beyond its evocation of dada and machine guns. As the poem advances, language itself begins to crack, fissure. Grammar loses its already loose hold, replaced by cartridges of the shout. Words are wildly misspelled; "close the prudentiatl burn the plicies." The power of the poem is revealed in this stress, revels in breakage, the language itself proves through its breakdown and splits the authenticity of the poem's message, its urgency. "it's nation ti eye ime." Language verging on gibberish, shrapnel, words torn apart in an embodiment of anger. "come out niggers niggers niggers come out." The oppressive weaponry of lexicon must be turned back on the oppressor, exploded, so the poem not only seeks to incite rebellion in society, it enacts rebellion in language. Burn, baby, burn. This rebellion, this desecration, nearly destroys what it makes, nearly pushes the poem over into babble and opacity, language that isn't language. But the poem doesn't have affect in spite of that stress-failure of language but because of it. Its volatility, its authority, even mastery are marked by its near self-destruction.

Hear that noise?

Edward Strickland writes in *American Composers,* "John Zorn is the most familiar, or notorious, composer of the New York avant-garde to come to public notice in the second half of the '80s. He is also among the most wildly syncretic composers ever." Zorn describes to his own style as sparagmatic, referring to the tearing apart of Dionysus. His work is characterized by quick switches between dramatically different musical idioms, blocks, he calls them, like Ives on crystal meth. Often these blocks startlingly oppose one another in mood, tone, tempo, instrumentation, and arrangement so that in a given Zorn piece one feels physically contradicted moment to moment. The force of his composition, its humor, terror, joy, and vengeance, comes from these sudden evocations and desecrations. His music doesn't advance so much as it accumulates. No way can his work be turned into elevator music.

In "Saigon Pickup," performed with his superband Naked City (Bill Frisell, guitar; Wayne Horvitz, keyboards; Fred Frith, bass; Joey Baron, drums; Yamataka Eye, vocals), I count seven blocks, each with a particular emotional valance and cultural association. The piece begins with delicate piano, drum brushes, and high hat, a synthesized violin and a haunting kind of hoot, which is half a girl's moan, half Zorn blowing through his disconnected sax mouthpiece. The effect is uneasy and sad, like hearing someone relive loss in a dream. The second block obliterates this quiescent mood with a down-and-dirty blues riff, grubby saxophone wails and Frisell's gritty electric guitar. The third block has a bouncy country-and-western bass line with some good-old-boy jamming. These blocks are then repeated followed by a fourth new block that is a jazz club piano, smooth and smoky solo trading off with guitar. The fifth block is noise: rip, scream, feedback. Then the sixth: a kind of early sixties rock'n'roll Hammond organ, a bit sloppy, stoned but comfortable, nostalgic. The seventh is hot, fast, straight-ahead jazz with Zorn playing a somewhat conventionally blistering sax solo.

Then the third, fifth, and first are repeated followed by the ending, which is a decay of the first block into spooky drone, muted siren, sounds becoming disconnected and distant. (You can see how when the band performed, they had sheet music, even though the music was as wild, free form, unpredictable, punked-out as imaginable—a theatric level of incongruity.) The power of this piece, aside from the excellence with blocks, how quickly and vividly they separate and define themselves, and the shock of their harsh juxtaposition, is that as a whole it puts the listener through a series of recognitions and emotions that conflict and contradict one another. Perfectly demonstrative of our confused and tragic involvement in Vietnam as evoked in the title: we move from sensitive haunted loner to cowboy to hepcat to stoned hippie to violent head banger, so that our identity, our involvement, is utterly conflicted, self-repulsive. We become, as listeners, obliterated by our own contradictory responses. We are a disaster without resolution, only fade-out, evacuation. As Zorn said in an interview, "It's put together in a style that causes questions to be asked rather than answered."

> "So that meaning can begin and in doing so be undone."
>
> —Ashbery

In Robert Hass's long poem "Berkeley Eclogue," a second combative voice interrogates, ridicules, prompts, and distracts the central voice of the poem.

> Sunlight on the streets in the afternoon
> and shadows on the faces in the open-air cafes.
> *What for?* Wrong question. You knock
> without knowing that you knocked. The door
> opens on a century of clouds and centuries
> of centuries of clouds. The bird sings
> among the toyons in the spring's diligence
> of rain. *And then what? Hand on your heart.*
> *Would you die for spring? What would you die for?*
> *Anything?*

It is no wonder that the bringing into awareness of creation as an act, as accomplished by a fallible, self-doubting creature, would lead to this sort of sparagmatic voice. This contradiction of singularity. Similar to William Carlos Williams's "Portrait of a Lady," which, tangled in its own figures of speech, leads to an "Agh," a frustration with trying both to describe accurately and to write a poem, "Berkeley Eclogue" doubles back on itself, aborts itself, undercuts and ridicules its own abilities to create effects, disturbs any sense the speaker has of being privileged, in control, an authority, the one who knows. "Ah, this is the part / where he parades his wound. He was a child." When images, the beginnings of narrative, a coherent attitude, sentiment, or mood begin to be asserted, each is hectored, exposed as a ploy or convention.

> Someone who heard you sing the moths, the apples,
> and they were—for sure they were, and good
> though over there. Gold hair. A lucky guy
> with a head on his shoulders, and all heart.
> *You can skip this part.* The moths, the apples,
> and the morning news. Apartheid, terror,
> boys in a jungle swagging guns. *Injustice*
> *in tropical climates is appalling,*
> *and it does do you credit to think so.*

As with Keats, the more the poet listens to the poem, the more it veers through self-loathing, bitterness, play, a fundamental suspicion of any representation of feeling or fact in writing as well as any coherent or singular vision of life. It is in renting, cutting, that "Berkeley Eclogue" demonstrates that self-consuming is self-generation. The series of negations, of challenges, does not cancel the poem out; the process of disagreement, of reversal, is productive whereas logically it should lead to silence. Inclusive rather than exclusive. ART MAKES THE WORLD BIGGER. "Then? Then, the truth is, then they fell in love. / Oh no. *Oh yes.* Big subject. *Big Subject.*" Indeed, each subject, each story, each lyric outburst has its shadow just as one voice is the shadow of the other, just as "shadow" is the aural and visual shadow of "subject." Each creation has its attendant negation, slash, the hand both writing and blotting out as it proceeds, simultaneously asserting and denying. This wedding/divorce of textual struggle and tearing with self-examination through memory embodies the twists and snarls of our most intense experiences. We move from emotion recollected in tranquillity to meditation in emergency, tacking. As Lily Briscoe thinks in *To the Lighthouse,* "Such was the complexity of things. For what happened to her, especially staying with the Ramsays, was to be made to feel violently two opposite things at the same time."

Stanza break.

Here are the 750–1,000 words on irreverence the Academy of American Poets asked me to write. I can hear your laughter from here. See what I mean? Irreverence is when something is where it shouldn't be. A new baby comes into the world and wails, in babeesh, What awful taste these people have! Mobiles full of pixies, a cosmology of fossil fuels. Its little fangs glisten. A Tristan Tzara the size of a football, it pees multicolorfully all over everything. First mind! First mind! ONLY THE EMPTY BELL RINGS. So you just go on from there raiding the golden sepulchers of the town dump. Have you even been to a library lately? They look like TV salesrooms. So I call my pal in Wellfleet who's received, ahem, special dispensation from the Academy of American Poets although since he's been going to Zen meditation a lot, he unnervingly oozes equilibrium and his skin has calmed down and he's always putting me on speakerphone when he's in the tub or under the blooming baobab. Just open your thieving, feral heart to the mortal stars, he says. No, he doesn't. Those are my words, and I'm selling them to the Academy of American Poets right now, yippee! I can feel the shrink-wrap upon me not unlike lion spittle. Really, though, only the dead should be allowed to be so much in their own world. What's a tanka without a tantrum? The rest of us mugs have to face up to the fact that flashbulbs are required to produce the greatest possible light flux (measured in lumens) in a fraction of a second. Oh Imagination! You just can't go off on your own with a Slinky. But go ahead, try. A pal of mine in Iowa says I'm a mainstream poet. One hundred fifty years ago, my second would be contacting his second, and I don't think it would go well for me, which is why I'm in this condition and it's barely three. Hurry up if you don't have the rhyme and if you do, too. *Hic.* Perhaps I'd been

discussing the student composition that was a cube
of misspelled words on fifteen pages in a row. Perhaps
I'm dog-paddling in the mainstream while one of the
atavists is lecturing about the work's pastoral project.
Hard to the stern: a teaching philosophy! Pah-leeze!
See page . . . Philosophers, when they stopped trying
to tell us the world was fire, lost touch with the body
and therefore with fatality, which gives everything its
beauty and shape and sadness. Tyger, tyger. Some got
to this river first and cried it. What a headache Zeus
had after Artemis pried herself out. Of course we're
abnormally interested in a poet's work when he or she
dies. It has come to an end! Leaves in a drained swim-
ming pool. That doesn't mean I want anyone to hurry
up and check out. Almost anyone. Theories about art
aren't art any more than description of an aphid is an
aphid. By splurges and splash, leaps and collapse, the
memory installs the past. The heart isn't grown on a
grid. I digress. Exit, pursued. Books of poems should
cost one dollar and fall apart as soon as you read them.
That's the only way I can solve my space problem. Hey,
I'm down here with the rest of the boiling cabbages.
Hello, Matt Hart. The proper use of a hammer is to
stand fifteen feet away and throw it at the nail. If you're
the hammer in the beginning, you've got to be the nail
by the end. Such is life, cowboy. If you go out the same
door you've come in, you haven't gone anywhere. Even

worms know that. The irreverent refuses transitional states; there is no between but like a quantum always here and there, such a perfect waitress. One if by whirlpool, two if by monster. And as such profane, heretical, because it doesn't observe the separations that pieties and sacred ritual insist on. The irreverent mixes. What we need is recklessness and an owl-shit outburst and a good smack upside the head every now and then. I, too, am a creature of electrified lint; give me a doily and I'll blow my nose on it, and I mean that in the best possible way. The poem is here to be defied. I almost typed "deified." When I typed "goof student" instead of "good student" in a letter of recommendation, it was very very hard to change. The irreverent welcomes its own desecration; it has no obligation to the truth (because there are too many to be obligated to), only to clear a possible space where new truth may appear. Sweeping, sweeping the temple steps is all you can do when hoping the god will appear. An onslaught of severalness within the asylum of singularity. He was driven crazy by the way people drive. The irreverent is the irrelevant's revenge. Inclusions are always the greatest risk. Skirmish of daffodils and dragonflies. The giraffes go knock-kneed to drink. Consistency is the triumph of insects. The irreverent is cracked in the plinth and therefore can sustain no monument, no argument, no politics. Surprisingly, some ducks have bigger penises than gorillas, and how do you think that goes over in the ape house? Do you doubt for an instant the ancient Greeks would have availed themselves of rhinoplasty and liposuction? The antidote to venom is venom, it's just a matter of context. Under the shroud, the thong. The irreverent can never be maintained, it's always its own debacle, in crisis of its own discovery and obsolescence. Stop me if you've heard this one. Can I get you a number of drinks? Inclusion is always the biggest risk. Coyote trots on the edge of the abyss. What can't be made more beautiful by an out-of-order sign? Finally, you can only trust yourself and you can't trust that nitwit either.

No doubt about it, since the dawn of creation, things have been getting worse. As long as I've been around, literature has been getting finished by television, itself, cheap gas, movies, itself, DVDs, the Internet, itself. The latest report the NEA blew a zillion bucks on before spending what was left over to get Iraq war vets to write sestinas tells us that no one in Texas has read a book in sixteen years. In Indiana, paragraphs are being drowned in gunny sacks. Haiku, once found running in the streams, is rotting on the shelf in Maine. What could this mean for poetry's audience? I don't care! I'm in agreement with the avant-garde position put forward by our dear, spotty Rimbaud that the audience is

hopelessly behind, always at best and worst a conserva-
tive force. To face an audience is to look backward. One
has an audience with a king, even the pope, but with
a poet? If there is an audience for poetry, it is an audience of privacy. Who isn't appalled to find someone else
standing in the poetry section of a bookstore? Please,
please let us not meet each other's eyes—although, fellow reader, I am glad you exist, even if you are drawn to
books written by numbskulls. Whenever I think of audience, I see one of those surgical theaters of the eigh-
teenth century. If the surgeon is particularly notorious
for being a bungler, the place is packed; if you faint,
you'll probably be held up by the crush. On stage, some
poor beggar's having something cut out. Take a look
at the instruments, Audience, a cross between minia-
ture mining tools and a gigantic sewing kit. Take a sniff.
Anesthetic? Doesn't exist yet beyond a couple of slugs of
rotgut. And the poor assistant holding the victim down
as the doctor pries and rips? There he is, Audience, to-
night's poet: John Keats because this is Guy's Hospital
in 1818. Now would you like to hear him read his re-
cent work? "A thing of beauty is a joy forever." Readings
are absurd and suspicious events but they are how,
in our current poetry world, we usually construe our
ideas about audience. Poetry, as everyone knows, is in
competition with girls' volleyball for the crowd. It's all
about numbers. Favoring performance (oh, surely there

is far too much acting in the world already), the reading takes place when no one is actually reading, just one hotshot mouthing off. In spite of the commendable ruckus and vitality of performance poetry, it is not literate. The performance of language is best appreciated in the isolation of a single receptive mind, much like the condition in which it is made. There's a lot of sulking these days about poetry's inability to speak to the masses, to address social and political concerns on a large scale similar to, say, *Desperate Housewives* and the NFL. And the great claims of the art's anemia when poetry speaks to other poets. Without going too far down the aromatherapy road of experimental writing, we can still say that poetry in a fundamental way endeavors to make the reader a poet. "Tintern Abbey" is a training manual. "You are my only reader and I wish to convert you," writes Hopkins to his friend Bridges. The song is always instruction in how to sing. And in regards to the common bellyache that the only audience for poetry is poets: but it's been noted by many that poetry is like a foreign language; you need to learn grammars and idioms to get it, so what's so terrible about people who know Portuguese being the people who are interested in listening to and reading Portuguese? Arcane specialization? Elitism? Surely no more than girls' volleyball. Poetry's greatest task is not to solidify groups or get the right people elected or moralize or broadcast; it is to foster a necessary privacy in which the imagination can flourish. Then we may have something to say to each other.

Meanwhile in the billiards room with a candlestick, desecration is the assertion of one mark over another yet the first remains visible. It does not exclude. It nears obliteration but if it erases, it does so poorly. It makes X a site of struggle not containment, birds not birdcages. There is always the next X. Desecration is the inclusion of what has been excluded, an impossibility. "I mean *Negative Capability*," you knew this was coming, didn't you? "that is when a man is capable of being in uncertainties, Mysteries, doubts, without any irritable reaching after fact and reason." (And one further textual uncertainty: the letter to his brother George in which Keats defines and names Negative Capability was one that came into possession of the man who married George's widow in America. Thinking these letters might bring some much-needed money, John Jeffrey transcribed them. Jeffrey himself was not literary, and Keats's letters were written fast, often crossed, full of hurried spelling mistakes. Jeffrey copied elsewhere "insolated verisimilatures" when Keats probably meant "isolated verisimilitude." So, given that the original is lost, it is possible that "Negative Capability" is not at all what Keats called his idea.) Desecration. The word is copied wrong, the margin charges the center. It is noise overwhelming music and becoming melodic. The word purified with error. The urinal hung in the gallery. Incoherence always attending. Opacity always attending. Non sequitur. The boats bobbed in the water. Ugliness. Storm incomprehensible and comprehensible simultaneously. Pay no attention to that man behind the curtain. Take a pair of scissors.

To be only comprehensible is to be fully known is to be already seen, predictable. The next poem must shake us, must wake us, must entice us toward the denied, the disallowed. It is what wasn't. Someone had erased a YES out of the charcoal Nos. The new is always scrawled over the old. Anything fully known offers us no site of entry, no site of escape, no site of desire. In the morning we mistook the roofers on the hill for flames. Desecration is the mix of opposites, that field of contact, the tear that draws us. "I think one could spend one's life having this desire to be in and outside at the same time . . . content is a glimpse," writes Willem de Kooning. Some of them chased each other, some of them fell to the ground. Coyote vanished into the smoke. The clash of the seen with the unseen, the broken seam, the unmasked with the masking that amazes us, sticky-out red thing, outrages and liberates us, embodies possibility. "We can't say things." But language too is a kind of materials, stuff; our next poem begins where we no longer handle language the same way. It seems both opacity and destruction are built into us, in our genes. Stretches of DNA are useless gibberish, there the code describes no protein. Jumping genes so called because they are preceded by a code that says, Jump over what's next. "Pay no attention to that man behind the curtain." "You can skip this part." But what's striking is that, for whatever evolutionary reason, these genes are there, they are included, faithfully copied in replication as if senselessness, as if all that was excluded from our metabolic logic is still a vital ingredient of our makeup. Molecular gerontologists are convinced that our cells are hardwired for mortality: there's also something in our makeup that includes its own negation, its own destruction. That's why poetry is about death. Perhaps our being in its wholeness requires demise, requires crossing out. I didn't know how alone I was until they brought out more chairs. Our lives are propped up by opacity and mortality the way trees are propped up by their shadows. Our flesh desecrates our mind. The next word desecrates the last.

Poetry is an art of beginnings and ends. You want middles, read novels. You want happy endings, read cookbooks. Not closure, word filched from self-help fuzzing the argument. The ever-grudge of love and endsville. I believe in scars and making scars shine. Kaput. Form is the shape of the selecting intelligence because time is running out. Form enacts fatality. To pretend otherwise is obfuscation, philosophical hubbub. A lie. We die. We go to art to learn the unlearnable, experience the un-experienceable. Art reports back. Form is the connect, primal haunt, carbon chain end-stopped. You can tell it's late because we prefer the songs of Orpheus after he's torn apart. Pattern as much a deficiency as a realization. No one gets to count forever. When you slice yourself open, you don't find a construct. Bloom rhyming with doom pretty much took care of Keats. Already I feel the flowers growing over me, he said, looking up at the daisy design on the ceiling. Wire in the monkey's diencephalon prints out a wave most beautiful. Open form prone to mouse droppings just as closed to suffocation. The river swims in the fish. The girl ties back her hair in a universal gesture. "The world of dew / is the world of dew / and yet, and yet" (Issa). A menu isn't a meal. "Put your trust in the inexhaustible nature of the murmur." Breton said that and know when to shut up, I'm saying that. We're not equations with hats. Nothing appears without an edge. There's nothing worse than a poem that doesn't stop. No one lives in a box. The heart isn't grown on a grid. The ship has sailed and the trail is shiny with dew. Door slam, howling in the wood, rumble strips before the toll booth. Enter: Fortinbras.

Ovipositor. Snow. Bam bam bam, let's get out of here.
What I know about form couldn't fill a thimble. What
form knows about me will be my end.

Hard to starboard: a teaching philosophy! We are all
trying, in the writing of poetry, to bring into being something that doesn't exist, that will surprise us, delight us
perhaps, instruct us perhaps, but we must always be
prepared for its initial unrecognizability. (Let me help
you, said the monkey, putting the fish safely up in a
tree.) Our concerns are with the products of the imagination, which is always, in its liberty, launching into the
unknown. "We can hope then in regard to what consti-
tutes the material and the manner of art, for a liberty
of unimaginable opulence" (Apollinaire). The imagination is that which will not be subservient to so-called
reality, so-called duty, not to expectation, requirement,
prerequisite, obligation. We are here to cultivate the
marvelous, to woo the new from yourselves, to com-
mune with otherness. There will be no music made from
chains except they be cast off. As critics of each other's
work we must be very careful making assumptions, con-
structing interpretations, and making recommendations
for revision before we actually know what it is we are
looking at. An emerald necklace is indeed a very poor
piece of birthday cake. I am very suspicious of the diag-
nostic model, that poems are evidence of sickness, of

deficiency, like lab reports the doctor looks over, then tells the young poet, Oh, your music-globin is dangerously low, take this Dylan Thomas for a week. You seem not to know how to shape a line; take a semester to write an essay about it and get back to me. ("You'll never catch a fish / that way, you said. One caught a fish that way.") Writing poetry isn't problem solving. Our primary job is description, to remark the places in this new work that are most intriguing, baffling, that seem most in dialogue with aspects of the tradition and most in revolt against it. What may seem like a mistake may in fact be the most important point in the poem, where the poet is trying to discover new territory, new methods and materials. "A man [and woman] of genius makes no errors. His [her] errors are . . . portals of discovery" (James Joyce). The imagination is forever in advance of criticism.

A few years ago Robert Hass said to me, I still don't know what I'm doing, at which point it occurred to me that not knowing what we're doing is obviously the thing to do. So how does one get better at not knowing what one is doing? This is where the feedback of the workshop can be crucial and vital; in workshop the products of a poet's not knowing can be examined and exposed, described so that what is successful for whatever reason (magical music, force of structure, variety of juxtaposition) dialogue with tradition can be brought into the light so they become part of the poet's conscious abilities, additions to a technical repertoire. As Eliot says in "Tradition and the Individual Talent," "The bad poet is usually unconscious where he ought to be conscious, and conscious where he ought to be unconscious." Forget Eliot's scolding manner, and substitute imagination for the unconscious; we can say that there is a vital exchange between them that takes place in poetry. The conscious mind can adopt the discoveries of the imagination and turn them into technical possibilities. But the imagination will not tolerate being known, mastered by the conscious for long, so it then leapfrogs further, and in this way the poet gets more sophisticated at not knowing what he or she is doing. The other condition can only be complacency, the greatest enemy of art. (It is also worth entertaining the notion that the least important time in any workshop is when your own work is being talked about. It's called "Poetry Workshop," not "Me Workshop," after all. The imagination wants to say something you can hear and often what you say about someone else's poem is really exactly what you need to hear about your own. The way in is to go out.)

Hard about! Errors may seem like mistakes because they have not been fully cultivated. Whatever happens in a poem must have repercussions, consequence from that point on. Whatever chance delivers must become crucial. "To tear the shirt and clean the soul is crucial. / What makes language is accidental" (Šalamun). Profligacy must assert fidelities. In early drafts, the assertion of chance, the welcoming of accident, comes from the permission of the divergent mind. But tack, take in contrary drafts. The centripetal Scylla needs to be countered by the centrifugal singular focus of Charybdis to realize form: form is achieved by exclusion; it marks an inside and outside; it asserts what does and does not belong and is counter to sprawling exploration. It is the inburst of outburst. Clarity results from the intensity of choice. Meaninglessness results not from too little but too much meaning. A string of randomly selected words is a site of nearly unlimited interpretations generating only vagaries because no decision has been made. Such choice may be to accentuate and discover the repercussions of error or to impose mathematic, prosodical limits. It may be instinctual or intentional, or, most likely, a collaboration between the sensed and known, body and mind, nerve and logic. Choice is most powerful when it is both made to seem inevitable, fated, and it occurs within a wide field of possibilities and somehow conveys the explosive anarchy of the universe in a single satellite's orbit. Don't build a reactor without a radiant core but don't produce a radiant core without providing containment. Freedom may be most keenly conveyed through struggle and tension, the nobilities of control in the proximity of chaos. Be buffeted by many winds; tack through many contrary drafts.

It may be possible that the dream you have while sleeping through class is more important than the class: Surrealism 101!

When Salvador Dalí came to the United States in the thirties and bizarrely decorated a Bonwit Teller department store window, earning himself the anagrammatic name from Breton of Avida Dollars, what was thought of as surreal became debased to a capitalist trifle. Fashion models wore lobsters on their heads, the rich gave dinner parties with pianos in trees. A few years ago, when one pop idol tore another's faux gladiatorial chest plate to expose a doubtlessly augmented breast during a Super Bowl halftime show, the media proclaimed the spectacle surreal. Even given the absurd replays on ESPN the next day, in stop-action, slow motion, and reverse, the avowed wardrobe malfunction between two millionaire vapidities cooked up to jolt a beer-bloated populace was about as erotic as a potato chip bag being ripped open and no more surreal than the ingredients list on the bag. Its shock was hardly fuel for the imagination and excited only a few censors, book burners, and televangelists to up the volume of their usual cant. On the other hand, an earlier event referred to again and again as surreal truly was: 9/11, and not only for the strangeness of the nightmarish visions it provided. One image, of people fleeing the scene, all members of a single united ash-colored race, is emblematic of the actual aims of Surrealism. For weeks afterward it seemed that this hideous trauma had so destabilized our habituated assumptions that we as a people were presented with the raw materials to bring about profound change, in consciousness and deed. Perhaps this shock, its attendant pain and empathetic flood, grief, outrage, worry, pride, dream could have been the starting point for political and social revolution, for the examination of our foreign and domestic policies and a reaffirmation of a humane attitude toward and in the world. Soon enough, however, the gorillas took over with their death of irony, death of complexity, and their fearmongering, and our failure is our complicity. More people in prisons. More lies and invasions. More advertisement for death, more rationalization of torture. But the surreal has always been and always will be with us, proposing sites for change. The movement that called itself Surrealism articulated and demonstrated that promise: that through trauma, confrontation, and destabilization we may be set free, that life isn't tawdry and the imagination is limitless in its power. Our peril is our possibility, the surreal insists, and its optimism is our right to hope that out of obscene negations something positive may come forth. Our poetry, as exploration, as fecund expression of what we don't know as much as what we do, has always been and will always be surreal.

Primitive, infantile, as well as intellectually perverse, Surrealism asserts erotic value based upon the efficacy of chance and the dreamed capacities of eruptive truth through whim, of artistic expression and random happenstance that take on the radiance of ritual. For Surrealism, the path toward a state of perpetual revolution is paradisiacal; its negative impulses intend to wipe clean the slate so that we may enter a tabula rasa of imaginative experience, of experience being imaginative. But the essential question in this path toward the marvelous remains troublesome: What next? How can the ongoing revolution of mind, of liberty of the imagination, be sustained and guaranteed when the means of that liberty eventually lend themselves to orthodoxy? How can recklessness be preserved?

But before we eulogize Surrealism, its possible exhaustion and/or necessity for resurrection, let's gaze back toward its origins.

Poem to Shout in the Ruins

Let's spit the two of us let's spit
On what we loved
On what we loved the two of us
Yes because this poem the two of us
Is a waltz tune and I imagine
What is dark and incomparable passing between us
Like a dialogue between mirrors abandoned
In a baggage-claim somewhere say Foligno
Or Bourboule in the Auvergne
Certain names are charged with distant thunder
. . .
Drunkenness sped my run through the martyred
      oaks
Which bled prophetically while day
Light fell mute over the blue trucks
I remember so many things
So many evenings rooms walks rages
So many stops in worthless places
Where in spite of everything the spirit of mystery
      rose up
Like the cry of a blind child in a remote train depot
. . .
So I am speaking to the past Go ahead and laugh
At the sound of my words if you feel that way

He loved and Was and Came and Caressed
And Waited and Kept watch on the stairs which
    creaked
Oh violence violence I am a haunted man
And waited and waited bottomless wells
I thought I would die waiting
Silence sharpened pencils in the street
A coughing taxi drove off to die in the dark
And waited and waited smothered voices
In front of the door the language of doors
Hiccup of houses and waited
One after another familiar objects took on
And waited the ghostlike look And waited
Of convicts And waited
And waited God Damn
Escaped from a prison of half-light and suddenly
No Stupid No
Idiot
The shoe crushed the nap of the rug
I barely return
And loved loved loved but you cannot know how
    much
And loved it's in the past
Loved loved loved loved loved
Oh violence
It's nothing but a joke to those
Who talk as if love were the story of a fling

Shit on all that pretence
. . .
Air a shadow in shade a name thrown out
That everything burns and you know deep down
That everything burns
And you say Let everything burn
And the sky is the taste of scattered sand
Love you bastards love for you
Is when you manage to sleep together
Manage to
. . .
The white rose dies like the red rose
What is it then that stirs me up to such a pitch
In these last words
The word last perhaps a word in which
Everything is cruel cruelly irreparable
And torn to shreds Word panther Word electric
Chair
The last word of love imagine that
And the last kiss and the last
Nonchalance
And the last sleep No kidding it's comic
. . .
Yes let's spit
On what we loved together
Let's spit on love
On our unmade beds

On our silence and on our mumbled words
On the stars even if they are
Your eyes
On the sun even if it is
Your teeth
On eternity even if it is
Your mouth
And on our love
Even if it is
Your love
Yes let's spit.

(translation by Geoffrey Young)

"Poem to Shout in the Ruins," by Louis Aragon, one of a circle of young French men gathered around André Breton who adopted Apollinaire's neologism, "surrealism," for their explorations of poetic procedures as life lived and lived life as poetic procedure, like many surrealist poems, lists in both senses of the word; it itemizes as well as lurches; its coherence is not a matter of linear development or consistency but rather one furious momentum through gushes and spinning in obsessional eddies. Its frenzy is both personal and political—a love affair gone sour with a you that is a particular person and a you that is the world, that souring even spreading to the very mechanisms of its own statement. Written after one pointless war and feeling the inevitability of another approaching, the poem's disgust and self-consuming revulsions of course have nothing to say to us now, to we who have resolved our own carnal stupidities and political obscenities. Aesthetically, the poem is a powerful avoidance of Eliotian anomie and defeat; even in its negative restoration of conventional associational tropes at the end, the speaker refuses to give up, to give in to exhaustion; if it approaches an elegiac timbre, it does so with blood on its teeth.

In Breton's rather unclassifiable prose account of a short affair with an indigent, mysterious woman, the eponymous Nadja, he writes of the modus operandi that he wishes to guide both his life and art: "I hope, in any case, that the presentation of some dozen observations of this order [chance encounters and events] as well as what follows will be of a nature to send some men rushing out into the street, after making them aware, if not of the non-existence, at least of the crucial inadequacy of any so-called categorical self-evaluation." With Breton's insistence on aleatory efficacy, he demonstrated a nonrational, antilogical way of reading the world and proceeding within it, a commitment and attention to an irregular system of signals that undermines conventional coherence ("all perfumes are connected by underground passageways") and replaces it with a personal, mythic, eroticized consequence. It is in chance encounter that he finds and forecasts "the event from which each of us is entitled to expect the revelation of his life's meaning."

The job is twofold: dismantling the habituated modes of enlightenment while creating and asserting a reactivity of imagination, a volatility of awareness and receptivity, a union of interpretive and active principles that are heretical, chance-derived, sexual, primitive, and profoundly artistic. Yet it is important to keep in mind that in its fundamental objectives Surrealism was not a mode of artistic production. Breton again and again throughout his writing expresses disdain for "the taint of literature"; even as he labors over his prose and poetry, he insists on the lightning strike of luminary and incinerating force. Art, both literary and visual, is instead a means to achieve surrealist goals: revolution of mind. But it is art, the materials of art that offer the best medium of provocation, havoc, and experimentation. Art is the laboratory results of surrealist activity, an activity that refuses to confine itself to the production of art. Poetry teaches a way to remain in a state of anarchy, which is perfect compensation for the miseries we must endure, Breton states in "The First Manifesto of Surrealism." While the aims of Surrealism were political, its involvement with the conventions of political action were conflicted and often absurd. Upon offering his services to the French Communist Party, Breton was insultingly assigned to write a report on Czechoslovakian milk production.

But wait a minute . . .

Approximately three-quarters of a century earlier, William Wordsworth describes a rather anticlimactic mountain climb in Book VI of *The Prelude*. After getting lost, he and his companion ask a passerby for directions:

> Hard of belief, we question'd him again,
> And all the answers which the Man return'd
> To our inquiries, in their sense and substance,
> translated by the feelings which we had
> Ended in this; that we had cross'd the Alps.

Wordsworth had missed the peak experience entirely. You climb the mountain, you have the expected experience climbing the mountain, that habituated commodification, right? Instead, what in *The Prelude* is a characteristic formal device to get Wordsworth out of all sorts of philosophical and narrative pickles, we get a stanza break then the ejaculation: "Imagination!" One way of reading this passage of a long poem subtitled "Growth of a Poet's Mind," is to see it as a critique of "real world" experience, of too much dependence upon experiential data in relation to logical outcome, suggesting that the real source of insight is in the energy of the imagination. "Life is elsewhere," Rimbaud will write in fifty years. Throughout, Romanticism's hunt for "the light of sense [that] / Goes out in flashes that have shewn to us / The invisible world" is in encounters with the irrational, be it Coleridge's famous narrator as voyager dropped off the map in "The Rime of the Ancient Mariner," or Keats bringing us to that liminal state of consciousness where dreaming and waking cannot be differentiated. In the "Preface to Lyrical Ballads," Wordsworth writes of the double task he and Coleridge shared—to make the usual unusual and the unusual usual, thereby opening the locks between the ordinary and the extraordinary, and illustrating ways of knowing and experiencing outside rational systems. Romanticism begins an investigation of the imagination that will reach full, monstrous results with Surrealism. Central to Romanticism is the power of the imagination, and many poems trace the process by which it is imperiled, found, revived, and released. As such, like much surrealist work, these poems function both as results of investigative methods and instruction manuals to those methods, very much a learn-by-doing system, the record of what happens serving as means to achieve imaginative liberation and wholeness of being, "a sense

sublime / Of something far more deeply interfused"
where "We see into the life of things," as Wordsworth
puts it in his great course outline, "Tintern Abbey." You
can in fact do it on your own at home, or trampling
about, perhaps one of the reasons Breton referred to
Romanticism as "the prehensile tail of Surrealism."

Cut to a precocious sixteen-year-old French schoolboy
writing on August 15, 1871, what would become known
as the "Letter of the Seer." It begins with a scathing in-
dictment of past literature: "man [was] not working to
develop himself, not yet awake, or not yet enveloped in
the fullness of the dream. Functionaries, writers: author, creator, poet—such a man never existed." Now of
course things were going to be different and "Poetry
will no longer beat *within* action: it *will be before* it."
Here is where the literal meaning of the avant-garde
begins to take shape; borrowing terms from the military, artists will be theorized again and again in the
early twentieth century as shock troops, and the casualties will be high; in fact, the height of the casualties
will in itself become a model of avant-gardist authenticity. Failure is a necessity of the heroic, confrontational terms the artist is conceived in. In this letter,
written to his schoolteacher, Rimbaud clearly sketched
out the principles of artistic activity and theory that
would so dramatically mark the next century. Identity

will become plastic even as the art is enacted upon the self. "For I is someone else. If brass wakes up a trumpet, it is not its fault." The freeing of the self towards larger visions requires violent disentanglement, negation of self and moral indebtedness. "If the old fools had not discovered the wrong meaning of the I, we would not have to sweep away those millions of skeletons who, for an infinite length of time, have accumulated the products of a one-eyed intelligence, shouting they were the authors!" Instead, the new artist must be forward-seeing so "The poet would define the amount of unknown awaking in his time"; he is dedicated to the new, willingly deformed. "The poet becomes a seer through a long, immense, and reasoned derangement of all the senses." The poet turns himself into a laboratory for and of the irrational in order to cultivate the unknown. Here come the monsters!

Flash forward to June 28, 1914. A Serbian national shoots the Austrian Archduke Francis Ferdinand, who bleeds to death from his wounds in part because he is so trussed up in his tight-fitting regalia, the blood is squeezed from his body. One month later, having declared war on Serbia, Austria-Hungary appeals to its ally Russia, who then progresses to a general mobilization by July 31, and through a system of alliances and reactions rivaling the absurd intricacies of a Rube Goldberg machine,

Europe heaves itself into war. "The plunge of civilization into this abyss of blood and darkness . . . is a thing that so gives away the whole long age during which we have supposed the world to be, with whatever abatement, gradually bettering," wrote Henry James.

In the beginning of World War I, Rupert Brooke could write of the blood of young soldiers as "The red / sweet wine of youth." Lord Northcliffe remarked of "young daredevils who . . . enter upon their task in a sporting spirit with the same cheery enthusiasm as they would show for football." Everyone goes off to war victorious after all. In fact, a few early engagements were begun by the English by kicking a football toward the enemy, but by 1916 the stench of corpses was reaching London and Paris and Zurich and Berlin, the progress of the conflict unclear, its objectives muddled. "Bent double, like old beggars under sacks, / Knock-kneed, coughing like hags, we cursed through sludge," begins Wilfred Owen's "Dulce Et Decorum Est," presenting a much grimmer, more realistic picture of the war where soldiers are impoverished, sick, emasculated, in retreat, confused. Owen himself was among the last casualties of that war, dying in a trench the day before armistice began, but after it had already been arranged for the symbolic hour of 11:00 a.m. on November 11, the eleventh hour of the eleventh day of the eleventh month, the consequent delay for the creation of yet another empty slogan killing Owen. In the Battle of the Somme, which would become known as the Great Fuck-up, through military incompetence, 60,000 of 110,000 troops were mowed down by machine guns during a single day. In the meantime, the English government issued a flyer called "What can I do? How the civilian can help the crisis. Be cheerful. Write encouraging letters to friends at the front. Don't spread foolish gossip. Don't think you know better than Haig" (the British field marshal). In other words, pretend, be patriotic, shut up, and trust us. Which is precisely what dada refused to do.

More dada? Da!

"The devising and raising of public hell was an essential function of any dada movement, whether its goal was pro-art, non-art, or anti-art. And when the public, like insects or bacteria, developed immunity to one kind of poison, we had to think of another," wrote Hans Richter of the movement. Bracketed between the suicide of Jacques Vache in 1919 and that of James Rigaut in 1929, both expressing through their self-inflicted deaths the ultimate nihilist statement of the pointlessness of life, dada was a multinational, variously valenced fit brought on by the murderous hypocrisy of the status quo. *Dada,* the word, is typical of the movement in that the naming is given various accounts but all are united in the sense that "it means nothing, aims to mean nothing, and was adapted precisely because of its absence of meaning. . . . Dada sweeps through the world not in spite of but because of its meaninglessness," wrote Richard Huelsenbeck. All dada's proponents shared a profound disgust with society, politics, and culture, and chose to make a celebration and debacle of that disgust. Primarily concerned with staging events, what we would now call performance art, the dadaists chose to promote outrage by outrageous, self-sabotaging mockery. "To be dada is to be against dada," concluded Tristan Tzara on and on. Here's a description of a typical dada soiree as recorded by ringleader Tzara: "In the presence of a compact crowd Tzara demonstrates, we demand the right to piss in different colors, Huelsenbeck demonstrates, Ball demonstrates . . . Janco . . . the dogs bay and the dissection of Panama on the piano and dock—shouted poem—shouting and fighting in the hall, first row approves second row declares itself incompetent to judge the rest shout, who is the strongest, the big drum is brought in, Huelsenbeck against 200 . . . people protest shout smash windowpanes . . . here come the police . . . Cubist dance . . ." Sounds like the usual military operation to me.

Gadji Beri Bimba

gadji beri bimba glandridi laula lonni cadori
gadjama gramma berida bimbala glandri galassassa
    laulitalomini
gadji beri bin blassa glassala laula lonni cadorsu
    sassala bim

. . .

(Hugo Ball)

"Everything happens in a completely idiotic way," explains Tzara. A true realism would show that "Madness and murder were rampant," as Hans Arp observed. The monstrosities of Hannah Höch's collages and George Grosz's caricatures mirrored the reconstructed faces and experimental prostheses clattering through the streets and propped in cafés like the toxed flotsam of a botched mass suicide. Dada was the century's first realism; it was the end of illusion in ultimate disillusionment. The cacophonous performances of simultaneously declaimed nonsense poems and piano pummelings and pictures drawn and immediately erased from blackboards differed from the snarl and smear of political posturings, tactical idiocies, and social lies only in that in dada no one got killed except by himself! Everyone was already limping anyway. "Revolted by the butchery of the 1914 World War, we devoted ourselves to the arts. . . . We were seeking art based on fundamentals, to cure the madness of the age," stated Arp. Or at least to trepan it.

Exhibit B: Man Ray's poem persists in frontal assault that makes the avant-garde pretensions of today seem like wormy appeals for tenure. Has he succeeded in writing a poem that reaches the most unlikely of goals: to be understood by all? Certainly the poem is written in a universal language. You don't even have to know how to read to read it! Even the translations I have seen, from French into Italian, in German and English, preserve all its effects; nothing is lost. Its measure and musicality remain unalterable. The poem reaches a level of originality that defeats ownership and individuality. Like the readymades of Man Ray's henchman Duchamp, the poem slips all our forms of authentification, confounding us in self-consuming confabulation of aesthetic judgment. To some degree, all poetry must create some degree of impenetrability; otherwise the words are mere indicators of things beyond them and, therefore, immediately dispensable, disposable. Some poets create opacity through excess luminosity, like Hopkins, whose stylistic wattage sets up impediments to getting at the poem's content. Man Ray's poem achieves opacity purely through an extremity of mark in a drenching of ink which irrationally becomes utterly lucid. All poetry is a form of encryptment and the reading of poetry is much like breaking a code. Here the code has achieved some sort of purity; it cannot be broken, yet the severity of encryption, its hiddenness, leads to lucidity. The inarticulatable is articulated. The poem is blunt in presenting a series of signs that stand for everything that is deleted, deferred, defeated, and cannot be divulged. Maybe there is nothing left in the graves of civilization worth exhuming. The message has already been cut from the doughboy's letter home because finally all information is too sensitive, subject to censor, or there is no message to send. This is the poem at the end of all poetry, when everything is crossed out, the ultimate revision, the perfected imperfection, the antipode to Mallarmé's perfect blank. Yet could it also be, not the interpolated outcome of revisionist zeal, a disowning of the past, but rather a recapitulation, an utter welcoming, the culmination of a culture building on itself, the last density that allows no escape? Shakespeare under Donne under Jonson under Herrick under Milton under Swift under Blake under Keats under Tennyson under Browning under under under. Or maybe it's just a dark, dumb joke.

Perhaps unsurprisingly, dada exhausted itself and its own poisons and ironies. A practice that insists upon the meaninglessness of itself, the fraud of art, and the pointlessness of life becomes either redundant or requires suicide as the ultimate theater. Versions of dada will continue to appear (fluxus, cobra, art brut) whenever new pieties become fixed ("meet the new boss, same as the old boss," goes a song by the Who, who, in their earlier practice of smashing their instruments after every show showed their dada stripes), but after a while even train wrecks become tedious. Punk goes corporate. Springing from the Paris dada group, however, the surrealists took dada's vigorous rupturing iconoclasm, preserving its unconditional outrage and love of scandal, and harnessed it to a rapture that is redemptive of the human condition primarily by accentuating and redefining the powers of the imagination.

In 1915, because of his meager medical training, André Breton was sent to the Saint-Dizier psychiatric center to aid "men who had been evacuated from the front for reasons of mental distress," he wrote in his journal. There he encountered, in the fabrications of the mad, "astonishing images on a higher plane than those which would occur to us," images that created an energy that seemed radiantly poetic. One patient Breton leaves a rather lengthy account of: "He was a young, well-educated man who, in the front lines, had aroused the concern of his superior officers by a recklessness carried to extremes: standing on the parapet in the midst of bombardments, he conducted the grenades flying by. . . . He supposed war was only a simulacrum, the make-believe shells could do no harm, the apparent injuries were only make-up! 'True,' the subject calmly states, 'I have stepped over corpses. They stock the dissection rooms with them. A good number more might have been made of wax.'"

What Breton admires here is the clarity of the imagination, its finesse in creating a convincing world, not its delusion. Breton knows as well as anyone that the war was an appalling fact, all the corpses real, but the horror of this fact was accentuated by the mad vividness of the patient's imaginative production. Here was an extremely powerful creative force that withstood and offered a counter to the war, seemingly nearly impervious to it, a recklessness that gave access to liberty. It proposed an alternative, an extreme measure to recover optimism, "the total recovery of our psychic force by a means which is nothing other than the dizzying descent into ourselves, the systematic illumination of hidden places."

THE LIBERTY BELL IS MORE CONVINCING WITH THE CRACK!

"I could spend my whole life prying loose the secrets of the insane," Breton will write in the "First Manifesto of Surrealism" nine years later, the single-most important aesthetic statement of the twentieth century. I do not mean to suggest Breton was alone in forming, fomenting, and spreading the principles and procedures of Surrealism. In fact most of the early, pivotal exploration and articulation is collaborative, and the importance of collectivity is a linchpin in the surrealist revolt. "Prisoners of drops of water, we are everlasting animals," begins the first surrealist text, *The Magnetic Fields,* jointly written by Breton and Philippe Soupault. But it is Breton alone who will so forcefully, through three manifestos, state and champion Surrealism's aims.

The argument of the first manifesto goes like this: Imagination is in "a state of slavery" because "Our brains are dulled by the incurable mania of wanting to make the unknown known." (To turn poetry into craft, for example.) Logic is at the center of the problem: "Experience itself has found itself increasingly circumscribed" through dependence upon logic and memory, which conspire to limit possibility through a habituated sense of confined consequence. Experience of the new is impossible; every grape broken against the roof of the mouth with the tongue is merely a sensation echoing the past, a figment of some previous, original grape. Much of Surrealism seeks to put us in a state Breton calls in a love poem "always for the first time." The debasement of the imagination brought about by the perpetual deferral of experience backward results in increasing alienation, the sense that one is befuddled and constantly wrong in one's life, a sense of impending doom, guilt, the impossibility of not making further mistakes and finally the inability to love. Sheesh. The imagination restores us to the faith in rashness, the conviction of the immediacy of our own possibility, the magical reactants every moment and encounter presents us, the genius of not knowing what we're doing. Yes, it takes courage even to leave the house if you know you could fall; we call it fall for good reason, fall from the cliff of stability but the alternative is to be a permanent shut-in, sipping a weaker and weaker broth. The imagination in this formation is fundamentally erotic as it finds itself in perpetual and ongoing mythos of orgasmic self-reformation through encounter with otherness. Even breaking a grape against the roof of our mouth and leaves sprout from our lips, our eyes fill with fire, we "put [our] trust in the inexhaustible nature of the murmur." The inventions of the mad and the unruly capacities of children all speak of the cardiac volcano of Surrealism, as does most importantly what is still alive in us, our capacity to dream. "The waking state," Breton declares, "I have no choice but to consider it a phenomenon of interference." He isn't suggesting that we should all close our eyes and walk into walls; that's a dada notion because it's what we're already doing anyway. For Surrealism, the dream state is a way to facilitate waking to imaginative actions that have efficacy in reality, but it's also important to keep in mind that this is a manifesto and, like all manifestos, it is a provocation, extreme in its polarizations, intending to be immoderate. Be still my heart! "Dreaming," he continues, "is not inferior to the sum of the moments of reality . . . The mind of the man who dreams is fully satisfied by what happens to him. The agonizing question of possibility is no longer pertinent." Dreaming is the enacting of the fantastical, perpetually in liberation of the powers of the imagination; its concerns are primary concerns, life, Eros not errors, and death; the dreamer is set free.

It is through surrealist procedures that this state of freedom from doubt recovered. "Surrealism is based on the belief in the superior reality of certain forms of previously neglected associations, in the omnipotence of dream, in the disinterested play of thought." "Everything is valid when it comes to obtaining the desired suddenness from certain associations." "Surrealism . . . the actual functioning of thought . . . in the absence of any control exercised by reason, exempt from any aesthetic or moral concern." What this meant in practice was a lot of automatic writing, dream dictation, speaking in trances, collaborations, exquisite corpses, blackening "some paper with a praiseworthy disdain for what might result from a literary point of view." The goal isn't art production, to market like sleeping drams, antidepressants, and boner pills for the masses (which pretty much describes the *New York Times* best-seller list); it is a change in consciousness. Much surrealist activity and the visual and written art that it generated attempt to create a breach in reality through trauma, imperiling our expectations of how art represents and responds to reality, and what that reality is. It is that split, that wound where Surrealism sets its marvelous greenhouse and guillotine. "The mind becomes aware of the limitless expanses wherein its desires are made manifest, where pros and cons are constantly consumed, where its obscurity does not betray it. It goes forward, borne by the images which enrapture it, which scarcely leave it time to blow upon the fire in its fingers. The most beautiful night of all, the lightning-filled night: day, compared to it, is darkness."

Perhaps the most familiar vehicle of Breton's lightning-filled night is the surrealist image. Reaching back to a phrase from Lautréamont, "as beautiful as the chance meeting of a sewing machine and an umbrella on an operating table," the surrealist image seeks to create and transmit by simultaneously hazarding disconnection and asserting reconnection, disconnecting a thing from its stagnated context, then providing another thing equally disenfranchised from the ordinary so that a spark can occur between them, creating a new eroticized context. "Wine is flowing with the sound of thunder," wrote Robert Desnos. "I describe objects and the material relationship of objects in such a way that none of our habituated concepts or feelings are necessarily linked to them," stated the Belgian painter René Magritte, who often titled his paintings by going to his neighborhood bar and asking his friends, who had not seen the works, to come up with curious phrases he would then use. While the imagery of Surrealism, two objects incongruously brought together or one object given irrational characteristics (like Dalí's infamous soft watches in *The Persistence of Memory*), is what Surrealism has most commonly been associated with, I want to stress that Surrealism is as much the field in which these surprising conjugations and illicit couplings occur. Surrealism is the operating table. When asked what that umbrella and sewing machine could possibly be doing, Max Ernst replied, making love, obviously.

THE SYNAPTIC CONNECTION IS A SEXUAL CONNECTION

"In all love there resides an outlaw principle, an irrepressible sense of delinquency, contempt for prohibitions and a taste for havoc" (Aragon). "Beauty will be convulsive or it will not be," ejaculated Breton in *Mad Love.*

> "Reciprocal love, the only kind that should concern us here, is what creates between unfamiliarity and habit, imagination and the conventional, faith and doubt, perception of the internal and external object.

It includes the kiss, the embrace, the problem, and an infinitely problematic outcome of the problem . . .

1. When the woman is on her back and the man lies on top of her it is the *cedilla.*
2. . . ."

This jointly written surrealist Kama Sutra by Breton and Paul Eluard from *The Immaculate Conception* suggests that all nameable objects correspond to the arrangement of bodies in sexual relation, all things participate in an orgiastic potentiality that is collaborative and transformational. Oh, happy grocery list! The life-affirming vulgarity (to use Frank O'Hara's phrase) of art is not that it promotes detachment but that it is proof of a pulse in the flood of detail, an ability of word and image to flush the nerves to the point of lubricity, producing physiological charge by way of transubstantiation of sign, word into flesh. "It seems to me that in a rigidly hierarchical society, sex—which respects no barriers and obeys no laws—can at any moment become an agent of chaos" (Breton).

Free Union

My wife whose hair is a brush fire
Whose thoughts are summer lightning
Whose waist is an hourglass

Whose waist is the waist of an otter caught in the
    teeth of a tiger
Whose mouth is a bright cockade with the fragrance
    of a star of the first magnitude
Whose teeth leave prints like the tracks of white mice
    over snow
Whose tongue is a stabbed wafer
. . .
My wife whose shoulders are champagne
. . .
My wife with eyes full of tears
With eyes that are purple armor and a magnetized
    needle
With eyes of savannahs
With eyes full of water to drink in prisons
My wife with eyes that are forests forever under the ax
My wife with eyes that are the equal of water and air
    and earth and fire

—Breton
(David Antin, translation)

Breton's "Free Union" marks both a high point for surrealist imagery and its formulaic decline. On one hand,
it is a dynamic tribute to the beauty of a woman, cele-
brating physical instability, Ovidian proliferation, and
connection to the natural world. Desire is perpetual

transformation. The poem seeks the rashness of sudden nudity, the explicitness of sexual tension through a variety of associations, suggesting an excited faceting in subjectivity. Compare it to the more conventional evocations and beauty and you can see how exceptional and new it is. But even before the poems ends, a modern reader, rather familiar with eyebrows that are nests of sparrows, grows a bit bored, a bit too clued into the system, and the imagery itself becomes mechanistic. Honey, you seem somewhere else, meaning that somewhere else is a stalled location, when somewhere-elsing is the perpetual goal. The appearance of a system conveys a commodification of the imagination; the system produces product predictable. Everyone knows that the female mantis will often devour the male's head during copulation but not that aside from giving her a nice snack, the headless male, once the brain has been removed, becomes a more ardent inseminator. The ganglion for mating, being in the abdomen, is no longer distracted by the brain's processing of external stimuli; it no longer matters if the lights are on or off or if the phone rings. I have often suspected that the blood necessary to achieve and sustain the human male erection is that which is otherwise employed in the brain, oh, happy unthinking! Surrealism is forever seeking to cut the head off so other ganglions can come into consciousness. I don't think this poem is a failure so much as an indication of the power and success of its method; it seems clichéd and predictable to us because as an artistic approach, its successes have been reiterated and broadcast. So now this raunchy, racy poem seems a bit quaint. But I want to insist upon its underlying commitment to disjunction, to misfit, to the inappropriate and incorrect as lasting and rich. The ongoing accumulation of analogies does not depend upon aptness, upon the similarity of comparisons, so much as create a charged environment of transformational possibility so that the misfits are as communicative as the more obvious fits. Disjunction may be the most important characteristic of twentieth-century art, explored and accentuated in every art form. From the early Cubist collages to the independence of dance from music, disjunction has been central to most twentieth-century art, including the major poetic works of high Modernism, be it the radical juxtapositions in "The Wasteland" and *The Cantos* or the more severe and playful semantic destabilizations of *Tender Buttons.* Disjunction, even, is central to our ideas of the self.

The fractured self, its representation and the notion that that fracturing is the source of art in general, was an overarching preoccupation of the twentieth century. One particular form of disjunction explored by Surrealism occurs in, is situated upon, subjectivity. I want to make

a distinction between ecstatic subjectivity and pathological subjectivity. Ecstatic subjectivity as articulated
and extended from Surrealism (although not exclusive
to it) takes the fragmentation of self as an opportunity
for energetic release as well as a vehicle for new, usually temporary reformation. For the surrealists, change
in consciousness did not have a static, finalizable goal;
it was not achieved so much as ongoing, an increased
volatility and receptivity, the making of instability into
a positive trait, a ready resource constantly renewing
the possibilities of life, self as fluidly imaginative. Disjunction signals psychic tectonics in which the destruc-
tive, the desecrating is inseparable from the generative.

This optimistic notion of subjectivity has been rather
eclipsed by the tragic disposition of Modernism, be it
Eliot's demonstration in "The Wasteland" of fragments
shored against ruin, a sense of a botched culture and
personal sterility in the face of overwhelming trauma
(no wonder he resorted to writing doggerel about cats
to cheer himself up), or Pound's heartrending admis-
sion of failure at the end of *The Cantos,* "That I lost my
center / fighting the world" (CXX) and "I cannot make
it cohere" (CXVI). The futility of existence is related to
the inability of identity, of subject, to take on the stability of authority and knowledge, of insight, to not be a
victim of itself, the jarring loose of the single vanishing

point meaning the vanishing of god. That victimization receives even fuller, more florid articulation in later generations, particularly in the formidable poetry of Robert Lowell, John Berryman, and Sylvia Plath. The situation is far more complex than I'm rendering here; Berryman's clowning must be considered, and Plath uses the fault lines in identity to explosive, reincarnating effects, but I think it's fair to say of these poets that the instabilities of identity their work explores are pathological, seen and presented as illness. "My mind is not right," Lowell states as plainly as possible. Literary theory, and its handmaiden, experimental poetry, again to wildly generalize, are in part a vigorous response to this fetishization and commodification of the psychologically imperiled self, tonically debunking the notion of subject entirely. The self, exposed as construct, is demoted to decentered mush; there is no subject, the word I is counterrevolutionary, and poems that pretend to relate an individual's experience are the patriarchal flimflam of capitalist lackeys. There are only texts. And the MLA Convention.

But to convince me the self is decentered is far from proving that the self does not exist. Decentered it may be, and needs to be, but so too is it constantly recentering. The self may in fact have too many centers, and that is the source of much of our psychological stress but also of our great diversion, our capacity for change, creativity, empathy, love, and joy. The blood may be fake but the bleeding's real. My self is constantly disrupted, constantly recentering, regrouping with each experience; when I meet one person's eyes, when I meet another's, how else account for that voltage in those eyes meeting? Rather than seeing that process as brittle, as cause for crack-up, it may be conducted as music, as lightning if we are limber and cultivate a nimble awareness and receptivity that welcome and exploit such occasions: an act of the imagination. The self is always under construction, it too is an aesthetic creation, and the world is always offering up materials for garden and blast. If there is divinity in us, it is in the process of allowing ourselves to unmake and remake ourselves.

A cartoon by Saul Steinberg shows a man at a drawing table. The line that his pencil is paused at the end of loops back and is, in fact, the line of the drawer's body: the drawing creates the artist who draws it.

EVERY POEM CREATES THE POET TO WRITE IT

"A poem is written by somebody who's not the poet and addressed to somebody who's not the reader. Who the poet is as opposed to his usual self is sort of interesting. Because the usual self is very often just the usual person, like anybody who has disappointments and delights and practices small treacheries and great fidelities. When I think about William Blake, I don't think about the one with pants on, the one who's walking around the corner. That's somebody else. It'd be interesting to make a kind of gallery of pictures of poets in real life, with their peculiar infirmities and good qualities and then you have the paintings of the poets writing soaring through the air" (Kenneth Koch).

"It is unheard of that a man should write so much about himself," Wordsworth complains about his ongoing poem, *The Prelude.* The autobiographical urge is basic to the need to write, but the nature of what autobiography is, is revolutionized by this poem, which Wordsworth will revise throughout his life and let go unpublished until after his death. But no wonder, everything is problematic about *The Prelude.* There are actually two, two at times substantially different, versions, the initial being far stranger, rawer, more irrational, and better than the later. Flushed with audacious brilliance, youthful extravagance, it fails as a unified work, but that does not necessarily mean it fails as a poem. It lacks dramatic coherence, a clearly linear progression through time, and striving for poetic, philosophical, and psychological coherence is what it's all about. But its failures to provide unity may in fact be more revealing and revelatory, more successfully demonstrative of personal and aesthetic struggles. The poem begins with a gust of present tense. Inspired, the poet feels a certainty in both his present condition and his forward momentum. The traditional evocation of the muse that alerts us to the shadow of epic structure is here one of a reconnection to a personal mythos, one embedded in nature. He is home after a long time away, reconnecting with a valued intimate, and feeling confident in his abilities as a poet, in a state where, as Ashbery describes it, "All things seem mention of themselves." But quickly the poem swings from its opening insistence on present tense ("I am free," "I cannot miss my way," "I am free") to begin the second stanza in past tense. The dilemma the poem proposes is not only an aesthetic problem but also a time problem. As Rimbaud will say, "I am someone else," here I am somewhere else. One position is the historic perspective of recollection; the other propulsive, it takes us through experience in the present, leads to the unknown (the sublime), and in lurches and jumps risks its very coherence. The propulsive mode is what eventuates sudden moments of paradigm endangerment, of the sense of the end of knowledge, of accelerating to a point beyond coherence, in fact nearly beyond articulation. "Imagination!" (it bears repeating). The purely expressive "Oh!" is used two times early in the work to indicate in part the disturbance of previous referential capacities not only giving way to but also inspiring an extravagance of poetic release. Again and again we are given instruction on how to have such experiences. The poem often seems like learning how to pilot an airplane so you can jump out of it. So there is the self of the past to be related in the poem's future, the self that is recollecting and as such employs a more stable language, and the more propulsive self that is pointing forward, ejaculatory and unruly. There is also a third self that is more explicitly proposed later in the poem that is the future self, the under-construction author of the great work *The Recluse* that *The Prelude* is prelude to, a work that will actually remain unrealized. As Wordsworth wrote in March 1804, "This poem will not be published these many years, and never during my lifetime, till I have finished a larger and more important work to which it is tributary."

The problem then for the author may be seen as a dramatic problem too; he must use the present tense to create suspense but he must also employ a retrospective, reporting voice to indicate the lasting ramifications and significance of events. The challenge then is in creating coherence.

> I had hopes
> Still higher, that with a frame of outward life,
> I might endure, might fix in a visible home

> Some portion of those phantoms of conceit
> That have been floating about so long
> And to such Being temperately deal forth
> The many feelings that oppress'd my heart.

The failure to achieve a stabilized coherence may be the poem's biggest failure, but in many ways it makes it a more sophisticated, living, throbbingly daring aesthetic construction of the self. "Proved on the pulses," as Keats will demand art must be. "It's better with the cracks." Perhaps the primary breach in coherence is the poem's episodic nature, the sections that don't link up, particularly the ones dealing with Wordsworth's Cambridge days, his time in London and France. The middle books of *The Prelude,* by no means coherent in themselves, refuse to be incorporated, tamed into aesthetic shapes that we could easily recognize as Romantic. Two examples: In Book VII, "Residence in London," Wordsworth presents himself as a sightseeing flaneur, fascinated by the vitality of low culture, attracted and horrified as he "now look'd upon the real scene . . . face to face, / Face after face; the string of dazzling Wares." This "world of life and life-like mockery," the intensely urban environment of London, does not lend itself to self-insight upon which the poem initially staked its claim, but rather divides the self, displaces it through perceptual overstimulation. The book begins with Wordsworth admitting to a six-year delay between completion of the previous book and this one's commencement. Inspiration has stopped, paralleling the failure of connection the book will demonstrate. The history of the poem is the history of the self. Even though the philosophical purpose of Wordsworth's aesthetic yearns toward, and in many cases achieves, a time-defying unity of vision and being, the poem as a whole indicates manifestations of a self that do not fit, but must be included because of the poetic accomplishments of the interruptive, odd, and unfitting sections. The mistakes are not erased! The poetic attraction of this book, and others, even while being contrary to any referential goal of consistency and coherence, has expressive power and therefore gives us perhaps a more problematic but nonetheless dimensioned portrait of the poet.

The other instance of poetic insurrection mentioned earlier occurs in Book IX, "Residence in France." Nearly the last half of this book is taken up with a story of a well-born youth knocking up "a bright maid," his father's predictable reaction, their flight, the boy's subsequent arrest during which he murders one of the arresting officers, etc., etc., until the maid goes off to a nunnery and he is left alone with the child, "which after a short time by some mistake / Or indiscretion of the Father, died." Sheesh. And if that kathunk isn't loud enough, we get this authorial disclaimer: "The Tale I fol-

low to its last recess / Of suffering or of peace, I know
not which; / Theirs be the blame who caused the woe,
not mine." Cut completely from the 1850 version, this
self-contained yarn, somewhat antiquated and quaint in
its telling and not exactly fresh in its dramatics, seems
to come from nowhere and go nowhere. But, as many
critics have suggested, the tale is there as psychological
place holder. It is in fact written over the actual entan-
glement with Annette Vallon, the woman Wordsworth
got pregnant and left behind in France, which belongs
in this spot in the poet's history. In that light, the later
excision of it marks a sort of final repression and desertion that is not nearly as interesting as this partial
repression. I think in the youthful experimental lunge
of his poem, Wordsworth encountered material of such
psychic and personal force, the absence of any aesthetic
structure or precedence with which to deal with such
material proved too much for him, making him write
this strange tale and attribute it not to his own imagination or experience. But we shouldn't fault Wordsworth
too much; he is acknowledging unknown territory.
Psychology hadn't even been invented yet, and certainly
poetry wasn't yet a site of personal and private disclosure of such sexual nature, nor the exploration of desire.
Just attempting to write in "the language of real men"
is so extraordinary, we should ever keep Wordsworth's
wreath fresh. His aesthetic trailblazing was doubtless

substantial, enough so to create a self that is fractured and chaotic even as it yearns for and achieves repeatedly moments of coherence. Poetry would never be the same. The self is several.

Backward march!

"Who's there?" begins the greatest knock-knock joke in literature. Identity as a fixed entity that persists through time as a coherent whole is derailed by the knock-knock joke, in that one answer of who is there sets up a particular set of assumptions which will be undermined by further inquiry. Dwayne who? Dwayne the tub, I'm dwowning. The near farcical opening of *Hamlet*, its nervous demand in the dark to "Stand and unfold yourself," is a demand that will never be met in the play. Instead we get secrecies, plots and counterplots, mistakes, interruptions, dissembling, misdirections. The matching of right words to right actions depends upon both a certainty of identity position and a certainty of field of action, never a real possibility, but in *Hamlet* laughably remote. Annie who? Annie thing you can do, I can do better. The clarity of separation, of distinction, of what is what has been made impossible by political reality (the death of one king and succession of another), social instability ("mirth in funeral, dirge in marriage"), and the personal (pressing guilt). Truth cannot be discovered directly, it must be eavesdropped upon, stabbed at in the dark (the stabbing at the ghost and Polonius's slapstick death being parallels), or hinted at through the mitigations of art (the play within the play). "Mousetraps and snares to catch woodcocks." "Your bait of falsehood take this carp of truth / and thus do we of wisdom and of reach / with windlasses and with assays of bias / by indirections find directions out." In a play in which everyone is telling everyone else what to do, Hamlet retains his liberty through a resistance to any sort of coherence of self by which he could be sensibly manipulated. Keith me and find out. He is out of control performatively. His initial understandable grief over the death of his father and his mother's subsequent remarriage, which destabilizes his position in court as well as setting off all sorts of pre-Freudian gusts, while hyperbolic, explodes into a debilitating insight into the corruption of nearly all human exchange and endeavor. His every utterance becomes corroded with irony, exacerbating his verbal dexterity, making him perhaps the greatest character who is always acting out of character, who is devoid of consistency. No one knows what he is going to do next. For example, after ending act 1 with a speech in response to his conversation with his father/ghost with this exhortation to action: "The time is out of joint. O cursed spite, / That ever I was born to set it right!" when we next see him in act 2, scene 2, he enters reading a book. Who IS this guy?

It is not that Hamlet cannot act. He is performing all the time. His first line, a pun, is delivered not to his fellow characters but to the audience. He is not particularly upset by his not achieving the crown after his father's death. He wants to remain free to act imaginatively, to explore his own interiority and engage in social play and flirtation. He wants to act without consequence. He doesn't want to die as a character in a tragedy. But it is consequence that dictates the type of play he must take a central part in, and also author, knowing that he is the eponymous character of the play he's in, its star, even as he undermines the play's tonal directions, accentuates comedy at uncomic moments, overacts, chews the scenery, out-Herods Herod while espousing both philosophical and theatrical codes that insist on and admire moderation. *Hamlet* is a tragedy because Hamlet finds himself in a predicament in which he must make acts that have consequence and that he feels repugnance toward, which turns the final dispensing of justice into a Grand guignol bloodbath of flubs. His two central acts before this slapstick slaughter at the end of the play are both mitigated and indirect, Polonius killed through a curtain (this most verbose, spin-doctoring of characters at last coming to the point both literally and figurative, his last line being "O, I am slain!") and the dispatching of college pals, Rosencrantz and Guildenstern by forged letter. Police stop telling these silly knock-knock jokes.

The instabilities Hamlet finds in himself, his genius in their exploration is poetic; it is the circumstances that force his identity from being ecstatic to pathological. Hamlet as a member of the avant-garde chooses to acerbate the instabilities rather than resist them, and he attempts again and again to have injustices addressed through the medium of art and performance rather than tragic action. He chooses to both be and not be; he becomes an avatar of contradiction, coming to a conclusion that only through chaos can some sort of resolution be achieved, some sort of peace. If there is a consolidating point in and for Hamlet it is that death reduces all. There is both consolation and horror in the notion, coming as it does in the broadly comic final scene. Hamlet cannot free himself of the contradictions and incoherences that bedevil him; they are his medium, through which he creates himself, but he can also not be fully their author or director; he is caught in a tragedy no matter his resistance, and finally he must submit to a final "truth" mouthed by a blustery blockhead Fortinbras that gets everything wrong. Hamlet was no soldier. Throughout, he is in revolt against the play he finds thrust upon him, and that is his heroic, comic resistance. As a character knowingly made of nothing but words, his means, caught in a snarl of assertion and denial, are poetic.

Hamlet's overrefracted reflections are primarily social phenomena; he is always onstage, and even his talking to himself is a performance. He has no inner life; his only privacy is in being misunderstood, and his self-making posits incoherence in response to a frustration and repugnance with continuity, the machinery that is both actual (his uncle's murder and replacement of his father) and imagined (his own revenge). Direction is impossible. For Hamlet, his artistic genius points out too many possibilities, puns too much, reflects on and off too many contrary surfaces so the outward manifestation of self-projection does not produce much more than a series of tantrums, self-consuming speeches, situational farces. Wordsworth's goal in self-making through aestheticized reflection is much more private; in fact, his resolve, direction, and sense of continuity are most in jeopardy in the books that find him in urban areas. Often after or during descriptions of Cambridge or London, he insists upon a return in his mind to nature and solitude, for a tonic sense of self-purpose, like a man grabbing for an oxygen mask, "Ill tutor'd for captivity." "Alas! alas! / In vain for such solemnity I looked; / Mine eyes were crossed by butterflies, ears vexed / by chattering popinjays; the inner heart seemed trivial," he proclaims. "Hush'd, meanwhile, was the under soul," and nature's instruction will reemerge, "teaching comprehension with delight, / And mingling playful with pathetic thought."

In both *Hamlet* and *The Prelude,* the inconsistencies of self, the challenges to the fixity of identity, are seen as negatives, even though it is in each case those very challenges that propel the work: they are integral to the poetry's power and to the identity's interest. In both cases, the main characters develop ruses and avoidances to negotiate incoherences and trauma, which in fact profitably traumatize the work itself and the work's creation of identity. But what would happen if a poem asserted a self by taking as given and as inspiration the heterogeneity of social constructs, emotional being, that took as its central notion a fluid, expanding, contradictory, inclusive nature of poetry and self?

I celebrate myself,
And what I assume you shall assume,
For every atom belonging to me as good belongs to you.

Walt Whitman's poem, like Wordsworth's, is concerned with achieving personal coherence through aesthetic coherence. But Whitman's aims are much less private. His vision, the vision the poem has of Walt Whitman, illustrates Emerson's notion that "art is the path of the creator to his work" even as it enlarges the romantic centrality of self to put forth a social vision that to some extent requires a constant dissolving and reestablishment of individuality. Also "Song of Myself" is the path of the work to its invented creator. Whitman gives aesthetic expression and formal enactment to possibilities of self-making, the self-made man, while insisting that the self is a manifestation and dependent upon interconnection with otherness. The great sprawl of this poem, ranging from somewhat loopy expressionist free verse to metaphoric collage, biblical incantation, Homeric listing, from narrative to the vaporously lyric, implicates us in a hegemonic spree of claims in its expansion of frontier both in terms of content and style.

"The poets of the kosmos advance through all interpositions and covering and turmoils and stratagems to first principles. They are of use," Whitman writes in "Democratic Vistas." One hundred years earlier Ben Franklin wrote, "To America one schoolmaster is worth a dozen poets, and the invention of a machine or the improvement of an implement is of more importance than a masterpiece of Raphael. . . . Nothing is good or beautiful but in the measure that it is useful." One of Whitman's greatest accomplishments was to take the private manifestation of self that was the lyric tradition and turn it inside out so that it becomes an insistence upon plenitude, national not private, upon identity by way of the poet the poem creates who is big enough to have such vision: Walt Whitman, kosmos. Social mission becomes personal mission becomes aesthetic mission in any order. The poem Whitman calls his "seething mess of materials" would lead to chaos (lack of form) if that seething wasn't demonstrated as pro-creative and generative to the poem's self-creation as well as the vitality of a nation. It makes for a wonder-fully elastic form, insisting as the poem does on other levels that self-realization is performative, imaginative, and that the self is not fixed, even as disclaimers serve to authenticate a goal beyond the text while, inversely, insisting upon aesthetic newness and primary expe-rience being within the poem. "View'd, today, from a point of view sufficiently over-arching, the problem of humanity all over the civilized world is social and reli-gious, and is to be finally met and treated by literature," he wrote. But even as he shares with Keats a therapeutic notion of the products and uses of the imagination, it is not a single point of view the poem presents us with, rather a plethora.

Whitman is able to make the expressive unrelatedness of his material referential to an ongoing self-making even as the poem leads to a self-unmaking, a dispersal of individual being into a departure that is also a welcome to meeting. In "Song of Myself," the poet the poem has made remains "untranslatable," "not a bit tamed," sounding a "barbaric yawp over the roofs of the world" even as he "depart[s] as air." The dissolution of identity is merely one more incantation of humble claim united with egotistical assumption: "If you want me again look for me under your boot-soles." How the poem achieves this, flaunts this contradiction of singularity and plural, self and other, is by exploiting a dispersive energy, the energy of incongruence that was the near ruination of *The Prelude*. The heterogeneity of "Song of Myself," of its formal experimentation and tonal swerves, is explicitly seen as an aspect of self-making American, a citizen of expanding frontiers, varied populations, scientific advances, and cultural gusto. "The United States themselves essentially is the great poem," he wrote in his 1855 preface to *Leaves of Grass.* The very nature of the poem and the social vitality it represents, its self-making, are explosive. "Do I contradict myself? / Very well then. . . . I contradict myself; / I am large. . . . I contain multitudes." The certainty of self is a certainty of otherness in the self. "Reality is the apparent absence of contradiction. The marvellous is the eruption of contradiction within the real" (Aragon).

Surrealism (Oarsman! Hard a-stern!) in picking up Rimbaud's notion that "I am another" and Marx's that "You must change your life," exerts a Whitmanian (Whitmaniacal) notion of the productive severalness of self to the point of privileging it over singularity, so that its art and aesthetics are based upon that which brings singularity to crisis through contradiction, refusal to observe traditional and habituated behaviors and distinctions, through transgression. Laughter, shock, sexual intrigue, the obscene, the radical assertions and dismantlements of chance are all means toward discovery of lost resources, of new declarations of rights and the provocation of the marvelous.

For Breton, the mad, like children and artists, have special access to the marvelous; they both embody it and perform it. *Nadja*, Breton's romance novel of his encounters with the marvelous and as such, to complete the transformational goal of surrealist theory, is an autobiography of contact with the marvelous that reflects the surreal self back. That's not a coherent self, it doesn't demonstrate an integration of historical event with a present that points toward future regularity so much as the sense of present molting and future possibility, a rift. There is no fidelity except to the electricity of perception and the undeniability of desire. The self that this set of aesthetic objectives creates is dependent for its authenticity upon future and ongoing transformation and finally serves not as a finished product so much as an introduction to and demonstration of a process. I KNOW MY POEMS ARE AUTOBIOGRAPHICAL, I JUST DON'T KNOW WHO THEY ARE ABOUT. "I am concerned with facts of quite unverifiable intrinsic value . . . with facts which may belong to the order of pure observation, but which on each occasion present all the appearances of a signal." Disruption, incoherence, rogue impulse are seen as signaling, not as a point of failure but as a promising realization of departure. "Leave everything / Leave Dada. / Leave your wife, leave your mistress. / Leave your hopes and fears. / Drop your kids in the middle of nowhere. / Leave the substance for the shadow. / Leave behind, if need be, your comfortable life and promising future. / Take to the highways" (Breton in *The Lost Steps*). *Nadja* ends with the abandonment of Nadja to her sorry fate, and Breton rhapsodizing his new love, "the Marvel, the Marvel in which, from the first page of this book to the last, my faith will certainly not have changed, there chimes in my ear a name which is no longer hers." "Who am I? If this once I were to rely on a proverb, then perhaps everything would amount to knowing whom I 'haunt,'" Breton began. The question of identity is a question of otherness. The word *haunt*, Breton goes on to explain, "makes me, still alive, play a ghostly part, evidently referring to what I must have ceased to be in order to be *who* I am." Not what you are, but what you have abandoned. Not a presence but a future intuition. Not the present, sedentary body, but the propulsive body, a voice.

The Voice of Robert Desnos

So like a flower and a current of air
the flow of water fleeting shadows
the smile glimpsed at midnight this excellent evening
so like every joy and every sadness
its midnight past lifting its naked body
    above belfries and poplars
. . .
I call tornadoes and hurricanes
storms typhoons cyclones
tidal waves
earthquakes
I call the smoke of volcanoes and the smoke of
    cigarettes

the rings of smoke from expensive cigars
I call lovers and loved ones
I call the living and the dead
I call gravediggers I call assassins
I call hangmen pilots bricklayers architects
assassins
I call the flesh
I call the one I love
I call the one I love
. . .
the earthquakes do not shake me but fade completely
    at my command
the smoke of volcanoes clothes me with its vapors
. . .
the assassins greet me
the hangmen invoke the revolution
invoke my voice
invoke my name
the pilots are guided by my eyes
the bricklayers are dizzied listening to me
the architects leave for the desert
the assassins bless me
flesh trembles when I call

the one I love is not listening
the one I love does not hear
the one I love does not answer.

The voice in "The Voice of Robert Desnos," the poet's identity, is composed by and of his capacity for calling, a performance of evoking. Supposedly taken down in dictation while Desnos was in a self-imposed trance, the poem's Whitmania insists on the ongoing exploration of self-making even as it ends in a sense of futility, unrequited. The self is sung into being; its tragedy is nonetheless buoyant, devoid of pathology; there is no sense of self-negating guilt or extermination; its recklessness is joyous even if it leads to failure; if there is a note of pointlessness, it's also the celebration of liberty from logical constraints, an encyclopedic romp that riots in the world of its own making. The optimism of every poem is that music is the solution, the resolution; that being finds its shape in the sung-so, not necessarily its completion but its expression. If we must end up unheard, there is still the frolic of the voice and getting drunken kisses from the cyclones it whips up.

Desnos's voice, like the voice in many surrealist poems, verges on self-eradication, you bet. There is not much in writing that rivals the power of the suicide note. Its last punctuation is of such insistent finality as to assert a formal integrity as irrefutable as a sonnet. Its language straddles the utterly personal and intimate with the hermetic, a language that converses with what is beyond itself. It refers both back, from a greater and greater distance, to those left behind of matters left behind, and forward with a conjectural implication that is by uncertain degrees dark and, if not joyous, at least released. There is nothing left out or incomplete about a suicide note; the notion is absurd; a suicide note of one word, that single word existing in radiant last form, in advance of its own definition, is always oversufficient, the message always finally delivered, full, indeed overfull, so that in the purest authorial absenting, there is a backwash of significance, it points back to babble. What is a poem but the management of silence and babble? The suicide note, as a form authenticated by ultimate sincerity, resides in the blessed state of perfect balance between silence and babble, between the perfections of nothing and everything at once. All that arises from the chaos of plentitude is brought into the luminous, harsh, final clarity of silence so that words lose their profane profligacy and duplicity and their inadequacy.

But is it not possible that the birth announcement too is a powerful form? Hello again, Walt Whitman. Can't the urge of greeting be as powerfully articulated as the elegiac and self-extinguishing that makes us want in some way every poem to be the last poem? Why not kill yourself? Surrealism attempted to answer that question ongoingly, through whatever measures necessary to announce the marvelous into life, risking, even welcoming the delivery of monsters to incarnate capacities dreamed of, to discover through the fecund profligacies of the imagination the erotics of every day. "Choose life instead of those prisms with no depth even if their colors are purer / Instead of this hour always hidden instead of these terrible vehicles of cold flame" (Breton). Perhaps the purpose of writing poetry is to maintain the spirit; be it through empathy and the amazement of finding ourselves unknowable, so strange it is a brilliance and glory. There are times when poetry's greatest task is to restore us to assumed things, but there is also its primary obligation to liberty, to the invention fantastical, to a series of wildly unsupported and unsupportable assertions that make life worth living at its more reckless.

THE RISK IS TO BE ALIVE

One of the powers of poetry is to bring us up to the unutterable and then go on speaking. As such it is always defiant excess, inappropriately jubilant even in its grief, flying in its despairs of gravity. The poet is like one of those cartoon characters who has stepped off the cliff only to remain suspended. But while the cartoon character's realization of his irrational predicament brings about its fall, for the poet imagination sustains this reckless position over the abyss; it is what extends the view. As readers, we are charmed by the postponement of our plummeting even as we are made aware of its inevitability. We are allowed respite above our obliteration—that's what poetry can give us, that renegade glimpse, a rest in ruin. The impossible is the first necessary condition of any faith. It is impossible to write poetry, therefore we do it. Without discipline. Discipline is good only for dispensing punishment. Sometimes the more impossible it is, the greater the debacle, the greater the poem. Just because a thing can't be done doesn't mean it can't be did. We all look into mirrors and see phantoms. Our error is our Eros. Why is there something instead of nothing? The answer is reckless and surreal. Who am I? Why am I here? What is this voice inside me that isn't me? What will be my conception? Why do I love? What will be my death? "Are you going to spend your entire life in this world / Half dead / Half asleep / Haven't you had enough of commonplaces yet?" (Aragon). Only dreams can rouse us. Each morning we wake with the obligatory liberty to conceptually recreate the world. We fail. There's some leftover energy from the first bang still causing trouble. We despair. We try again. We try to refuse a destiny of advertising and pennies and murder. "When the traveler loses his way in the will-o-wisps / More broken than the lines in old people's foreheads / And lies down on the moving earth / The wandering horses appear / When a young girl lies at the foot of a birch and waits / The wandering horses appear" (Desnos). The signal fades in and out, it is only intermittent, but our art may mark it, not as a tomb, but as a guidepost, a monument to toppling, a momentum, a moment of doubtlessness, which is impossible, of being touched, which is impossible, genius which is impossible, being alive, which is impossible.

The Decoration Committee

A poem telling the story of a man shooting a moose
is a narrative poem.
If the poem goes on for a long time and the moose
turns out to be his daughter who got screwed
by the lecherous, jealous gods and the man
then founds a city, it is an epic.
Many say the Age of the Epic is behind us,
the rain falls upon the moose corpse
and the murderous, capricious gods seem done with us,
killed or wandered off, and, unattended,
unhoused, we charge through the bracken
with only the burning hoofprint of human love
upon us. Perhaps the long poem you struggle with
is just a long poem as a big storm
need not be a hurricane. When I was a child,

hurricanes, like battleships, were given
exclusively women's names. Advances
have been made and hurricane Dean currently
is rampaging through Jamaica, an island already
wracked with poor prenatal care. There is still much
so much to do. Each is alone, shorn and bleeding
of lip, mouth crammed with feathers, hands full
of torn lace, the curtain rising on all
the people who murdered and loved each other
now bowing arm in arm. A conductor appears,
balding, and the crowd disperses to cafes
to argue and woo. How to know what now
to do, where move, what does and doesn't
belong here in a place we've been a hundred times
but never noticed the pictures of burning
buildings on the walls. Oh, what was once
a forest is no longer a forest, what was once
a tree is now a wheel. A poem, usually shortish,
which begins, "When I was a child" or
goes on about clouds or trees or lost love:
woe, woe, etc. is a lyric poem. The original
lyre was made from a hollowed-out tortoise shell.
From the tortoise's point of view,
the lyric was a complete catastrophe
but it has done very well by humans although
I know of no studies concerning and in how many cases
the lyric poem eases heartache by initiating 1.

the beloved's return, the door flies open,
the bra unstrapped, the moose dappled
with dew and/or 2. a getting-over-it
happiness at just having written/read the poem
which is about misery in the old way
but also in a new way and then noticing
the pretty barmaid. How little
we know of Sappho beyond the eloquent
snips of limb-loosening Eros. Chervil,
a spice, is mentioned for tenderness.
Other examples abound.
Robert Frost's "Stopping by Woods
on a Snowy Evening" is thought by many
to be a poem about Santa Claus, by others
suicide. Generally, the suicide people
have higher degrees. Anguish seems endless.
The heart however is often frivolous
perhaps as a form of defense
akin to the gaudy coloration of the tender
poison arrow frog. I am beautiful therefore
invulnerable i.e. deadly is the message of its body.
In English, there appears to be no rhyme
for "orange" but new words, like spaz
are being made all the time.
Many poems fill many books
and in this they resemble the records
of small claims courts. If towards the end,

you write, "Enter Fortinbras," be careful,
you may have written Hamlet which
has already been done. One of the ways
new kinds of poems may be written
is by finding out what people agree is not poetry
and doing that. Where are the timorous mortals
banged by gods? Where are the trees and woe?
Dr. Johnson, referring to a disease of sheep,
said that some subjects cannot be made poetic
but then along came the French.
Perhaps it was Ben, I often mix up my Johnsons.
After hours of voodoo drumming, everything
you do may seem like a poem.
You yourself may be what your poem creates
like a recipe will create a pineapple upside-down cake.
Poems cannot be "fixed."
Not like a dog, not like a broken motor.
If at the end only a few people are dead
and the rest mill about the fountains
as if waiting for a wedding, it is a comedy.
Who are the bride and groom? Maybe me,
maybe you. Who cares? Let the doors
burst open upon worlds of light, dogs chasing
brooms, the moose out there somewhere braying
for its mate. Is it not nearly enough to sway
to the invisible music, to watch the wrinkly
waters? To feel within the heart the crushed ball
of aluminum foil?

"In poetry the language of doubt must be written in
doubt-free language."

—Bakhtin

I was hoping that at some point I would figure out
what this book is about—maybe you are too. We began
where we began, with the primitive, and there we shall
end; the owl hoot takes a while to get answered across
the hills but it does. The primary urge to make poems is
connected to our most exorbitant claims of our power
and divinity, as well as our being a part of the animal,
mineral world. We are prisoners of raindrops set free by
our own flames. It is not that the intellect is an encum-
brance to writing with vitality, but I know overthinking
is the ruin of imagination, it kills off the volition of the
spark. The emphasis on craft, on a series of procedures
and techniques, is too much like the creation of perfectly safe nuclear reactors without acknowledging the
necessity of radioactive matter for the core.

Writing poetry—so silly only a human life could depend upon it! I feel no fear or particular awe for the
blank page (yet another postmodern sentimentalism);
if you get your nose out of cyberspace and actually look
at any paper, you can see its irregularities, it's not blank,
its fibers are flattened and glued mush; its imperfec-
tions are not imperfect, they are indications of a song
that is already there, differences, what makes matter

matter. There are no mistakes, there are only failures of recognition. All problems can be solved musically. On one of those umpteen Miles Davis box sets, there are three takes of a single song: in the first Coltrane hits an obviously off note, a clam it's called in the recording industry, in the second take he hits it again, at a different point, augments it, chooses it, this is Coltrane, man, so by the third time, it's not a wrong note, it's an integral part of the joyous soul-remaking power of his solo. The intellect moves us too surely and easily to self-hating and the perfection of death. Life, my friends, is a mess. Mistakes aren't contaminants any more than conception is an infection. Fucked up before I got here, fucked up while I hung around, fucked up when I'm gone. Good news!

Often what we do together to address poetry is muster criticism, all to the betterment of the sophistication of our discourse yes, but we are often in danger of letting that criticism eclipse the actual poem. POETRY IS ALWAYS IN ADVANCE OF CRITICISM! A poetic, interesting in itself, doesn't necessarily generate interesting poems. We must maintain a suspicion toward any system outside the incarnate poem that pretends to know everything about it. We must be unruly even as we acknowledge the worth of convention. Writing may be writing as the Language poets would have us think, but writing is not necessarily poetry unless it enters into a felt, assertive, reactive, embracing, and resisting relationship with convention. Experimental poetry's fetishization of the new leads to the depthlessness of novelty and the scarification of amazement. Convention is not necessarily conventional, and it is the obligation of each poem, at liberty, to show why. We have predecessors; I have tried to bow a little to some of mine here. When someone tells you you must learn other languages, forget your own. When told the self is a construct, bleed. The sonnet is dead, laugh in fourteen lines of iambic pentameter. The instance of now is upon us utterly new, we need not try to remake the telescope to see with it, it might be enough just to look through the wrong end. When someone says metaphor is fascism, run. When someone says you must address atrocity or politics or social injustice to write poetry, write in spite of it.

We forget that language is the province of fact and faith. We forget the basics, occlude the primary. We think the mask is the person and the person is a center of descriptive gravity. Maybe so, maybe so. But who does not feel some tragic falling off from childhood, who doesn't sense an unbridgeable alienation between ourselves and the world? Who doesn't awake powerless and take refuge even in his or her inconsequentiality?

That our poems speak to no one, not even fully to ourselves? That we manipulate codes about the affairs of manikins, traffic in densities without gems, opacities without anything hidden to be revealed or fall into the insidious rut of complacent manufacture? That we will never be naked? Have we even given up our despair of being of any use? Satisfied with the most minor of denaturing experiments, the whitening of an egg white when we could have the sun in our fists, five commas in a row when we could trade eyes with the jackal, craft elements when we could be clobbered by angels. Have we grown so jaded and empty to the word? Can't we do something?

Poetry is not a discipline. It is a hunger, a revolt, a drive, a mash note, a fright, a tantrum, a grief, a hoax, a debacle, an application, an affect. It is a collaboration: the bad news may be that we are never entirely in control but the good news is that we collaborate with a genius—the language! We cannot make the gods come, all we can do is sweep the steps of the temple and thus we sit down to our desks. When art strives for the decorums of craft, it withers to table manners during a famine. The job of poetry is to project emotions and thoughts, not eulogize them, not to inter them but to prove with ardent intensity what those feelings and thoughts aspire toward, flee from, that ring true to the apparatus of sensation and the medium—emotions and inklings that everyone has but through the extremity and enacting of poetry seem to have never happened before. MORE WRECK! I am not interested in the page that seeks to impress me by the splatter marks of brow sweat. The anemic and timid that masks itself in the veneer of prosodic perfection or in the dry ice fog of experimentation. Procedures on the right! Procedures on the left! Tack, tack. Must we remain perpetually unhouseled, unannealed, irreconciled with the worm and the thrush? The mind is an organ not to be defrauded with punishment. Whatever else the primitive is, I know it reasserts itself to us/in us through radical distrusts of any intellectual palace, parlance, or convention slogan. It will not be lulled by a jingle. The primitive reasserts itself with the immediacy of flesh. It may even be the recovery of sincerity. It may appear as a critique but moving toward magical assertion. It attempts to override the alienation that is the result of reified modes of representation based upon the commodification and capitalist refashioning of fake epiphany, you're absolutely right, Herr Professor. Our lives are not something we must buy and cannot afford. Our lives are free to spend a thousand times and we are never in debt.

I make these claims not as correct but as corrective, in the luxury of knowing I will be disagreed with. My argument is abandon and tells me to abandon every argument. I hope to come from a position of tolerance because generalizations always skip the vital rogue data.

There is no single, true battlement from which one can take in all the considerations of how and why poems are written. I am wrong, what a relief. My claims will always fail to take in the full diversity of poetry's instigation, inspiration, praxis, and aims. At best this has been my foreshortened, grotesque, unavoidably exclusionary of the very heterodox practices that enlarge and invigorate poetry, that advance it into abundance, that meet its age and future.

But I humbly submit that there are distinctions still to be made (he said, destroying any hope he was about to shut up). Form itself is a matter of exclusion. Art is the presence of one mark above another, decisions about what is inside, what outside. Poetry is the manifestation of decisiveness and affect within a charged field. Of course the form may be highly permeable like the cell wall or tight as a geode. Perforations as well as the reassertion of the previously perforated have always been a source of poetry; as has violation and transgression as well as the rebuilt and seawalled. Discernment is the accomplishment of the intelligence that is of most use to the imagination. The poststructuralist notion that a word is forever falling short of the world, of the thing, is more sentimental bunk. As anyone notices walking through the spring woods with a wildflower guide, classification and identification are far from a falling off; they enlarge the world: LANGUAGE AIDS

PROLIFERATION AND VARIATION. The separation of one particular from the undifferentiated green mass does not diminish it, it lends us vision. We can see what flowers are at our feet!

Let us review. How do we begin our lives as poets? For many, in the early delight that a series of syllables and/ or cryptic marks on a page can refer to the world, and not only the world as we find it but as we create it. The whims of the imagination! I remember a keen sense of the absurdity of language's relation to reality when I found out, it took days to believe it, that there had actually been a president with the silly, obviously made-up name of Calvin Coolidge. What better proof of a craziness of the highest order that such a buffoonery of sounds could occupy the highest office in the land? I still get the giggles when I hear the word *bosom* and was transported for weeks when I first found out what it meant. I'm talking third grade.

Writing Poetry

Writing poems is fun,
All the Clouds saying
Come on,
Think up something good!

—*Dustin Eggink*

All third graders are surrealists, saboteurs, reckless, ready to plunge into the deepest abyss, laughing. Their hearts are kites flown trailing a hundred tongues. Their language capacities are growing at an extraordinary rate, they have a conviction in the power of language, they know it can get them into and out of trouble. Language is a device with which they can probe the world's exfoliation of detail and stroke the whiskers of the dream. They are at liberty with its intoxications. After third grade the terrors of social life, of trying to fit in, begins to hinder that expressive range, their crazy what-the-hell zeal—why not make a rabbit talk?—their sense of the singing in the word is tramped down by the responsibility to refer to the clichéd and the acceptable. They are more and more orphaned from their primal urges. They become socialized, a word that could kill any glee. Poetry, if anything, becomes more and more a private record of privations, taking as its great subject isolation at the expense of any greeting or praise, poems about being all alone, the impossibility of being understood, of being unloved, unanswered, of feelings that the world greets coarsely if at all. The humility of writing poetry is made into a humiliation, and its capacity for intimacy is coupled with its inability to be heard.

This timeline is rather simplistic, I know, but I want to say that we begin as poets with extraordinary, joyous power in the delight of words and then find ourselves far away from the notion that singing can make the world ("One fish, Two fish, Red fish, Blue fish"); the poem cries out to and retreats from an insensitive world that will have no part of us. Scylla and Charybdis. Tack, tack. Let us continue to believe in the world-making energies of our sensitivity embodied in language, in the imagination, even as we must guide ourselves too by the self-extinguishing frustrations that our words mean nothing, and that the me those words create is of no matter.

But the greatest trauma, the necessary wounding that any poet must undergo, is the detachment from her own work. The beginning after the beginning. We must cut ourselves out and off to move toward a sophisticated sense of the art beyond our sense of self, to develop a historical sense, to see that we write in dialogue with the poetry of the past, to see poems as things, material to be manipulated. This is the big divide, what must be stressed again and again and not just in undergraduate workshops. We must risk a loss of passionate connection to distance ourselves from our work, to grow a little cold to it in order to revise, in order to look at a poem as a series of decisions. Why this and not that? We must develop an ability to read our own work skeptically. At this point, we insist on writing being a series of devices, be it Viktor Shklovsky's notion that in a work of art "blood" is there only to rhyme with "mud" or Eliot's depersonalization so the events of one's life are understood as material to be manipulated no differently than bending tin. We must develop a glacial remove, risking a fundamental estrangement from our work and our visceral relationship to it to get anywhere.

BUT

> "One detects creative power by its capacity to conquer one's detachment."
>
> —Marianne Moore

That condition of estrangement is extraordinarily productive, it is craft after all; in fact, it sites itself upon production to near elimination of the personal, emotive, resistant, explosive, primitive, and blooded. Its means elevate a mechanics, the caliper, le mot juste, mathematics, its choices often predetermined before any actual writing. Detachment says I know what a poem is and you ain't it. We have instead of the living nerve, procedures and projects. The use of computers to eliminate the human contaminate. I delight in John Cage, in his saying, "I have nothing to say and I am saying it and that is poetry." But alas I have been imprinted with a scream. I need to know almost nothing to fall in love but that is very different than knowing nothing. Cage's exploration of materials and aesthetic assumptions were corrective to stale emotional excesses and simplistic notions of self and poems. How wonderful to throw a bunch of screws under the piano's lid! But the personal presence, smudge that it can be, is what we always search for. It is how art companions us. For the OULIPIANS, a group of writers who positioned themselves in direct opposition to the surrealists, we are all rats in a cage, and their work, based on ingenious and wildly complex and mathematical restrictions (the most famous is Georges Perec's novel *A Void* in which the letter "e" does not appear, the novel being in part a mystery about the disappearance of an unnamed character—get it?), was an instance of the rats designing their own cage. Thus we are all seen as caught in constructs and our only sensible response is to manipulate those constructs. The OULIPIANS make hilarious hay from an entirely defeatist notion. As productive as procedural approaches are to poetry, as diverting and instructive of that traumatic detachment, they finally fall very short, they tell us nothing of life. Computers no more write poems than pencils do. Such a foolish act, the writing of poetry, only a human life can depend upon it. We must write as García Lorca said, as if we were about to be devoured by ants.

"You've buttered your bread, now sleep in it."

—Oliver Wendell Holmes

We must not take refuge in our poetry having no consequence even though one of its great resources is in the breaking free from consequence. Hamlet, poor fellow, sought a prolonged life of the imagination (almost as if he wanted to get a second MFA!); he wanted an identity that was malleable in play, brilliant with poetic facility, but circumstances demanded from him behavior that had the sort of consequence that perpetuates violence. He was no soldier, nor was meant to be; soldiers march in straight lines to premeditated mayhem. The zigzag joy of Hamlet's psyche grows pathological because his imagination's cultivation of incoherence in authoring himself is trapped by foul circumstance. The rifts in being that are revealed through and reveled in by poetic practice, productive of shifts in consciousness as well as discordances, lead Wordsworth to some of the most glorious moments in *The Prelude* yet also to his sense of its incompletion, immaturity, and failure, both the poet's and the poem's undoing, its desecration. For Whitman, such rifts and incongruities are embraced as productive differences; his self-authoring is ever-expansive (even his death envisioned at the end of "Song of Myself" is a grand, outward dispersal) and fundamentally healthy. Surrealism must accentuate the rift, occasion it again and again, so consciousness may perpetually reform and life be led with the imagination as its foremost sensory organ. Catabolism as well as anabolism conveys the full swipe and swing of being, its affect. What we write has consequence; within itself each word must be consequence of those before it, crucial, the onslaught orchestrated, and what we write must have consequence upon ourselves as we write it, as joy, as discovery, as growth in consciousness and the making bigger of the world. The consequence of poetry is in its realization of liberty, and its connection to the fundamental human drama, that country-and-western song. It has no debt. Its relation to the past is the desire to know more and more deeply the enormous number of poets who have gotten to the party previously, whom we have so much to learn from, to love and defy. We are not in a tragedy necessarily, even though, yes, we are all mortal meat. But we are feral, we lash and burn. In the beginning Coyote sung us into being. Our being goes on because we sing it anew.

We are all reading by flashlight during a power outage caused by the storm we are in, the storm we make and are made of. What we write must be worth those last moments of the battery's life to our reader. Finally I am not sustained by poetries whose electricity is not neural. The kind of poetry that belies mortality through the eternities of hyperspace, through the Google search, is of no use. Poetry is not information. Information is a corpse. Poetry is alive because it knows it is mortal. A poem is a manifestation of affect, of life, desperate life.

As vital as detachment is, if we allow poetry to be solely a mode of further and further remove, to discount the hunger and mad loves of self, the cliff dives of remorse, sacrifice rage to preserve the vase, deny the glorious eros of error, and replace the irregular heartbeat with a metronome, the result is emaciation, a rigor that leads only to rigor mortis. The continuous necessity and obligation are to reconnect, to break through detachment and its numbing alienations back to the fundamental synaptic mad hopping hope, the life of poetry, its primal surge, where we truly begin again and again. Not information. A twitching, a reveling in impulse, mortal being aspiring for the everlasting, in too big of a hurry to last forever or to go on forever but refusing to abide in the cold embalming of arithmetic or criticism's comfortable columbarium. The assertion of form is an assertion of mortality. Poetry is defined by its coming to an end. Poetry is yeasty proof of human life, record, and creation; its liberties and the liberties of flesh that the intellect, always telling us how far off we are, smashes against. The primitive breaks through logic like a foxglove through asphalt; the body breaks through the idea, a cry, a foot slam, a wreck we walk away from amazed.

Maybe tomorrow will be the day everyone wakes up to write a poem. Or maybe just you and me, fallen asleep on duty, fallen asleep to duty forever. No one knows what will happen, but you and I at least, while the music of a murmur invents us, will have no part in anyone's war, we will waste nothing, a signal going through us like an inkling of god or a hunger for strawberries or the indisputable fact of love.

Permission Acknowledgments

DEAN YOUNG is the author of nine collections of poetry, including *Primitive Mentor, embryoyo,* and *elegy on toy piano,* which was a finalist for the Pulitzer Prize. *The Art of Recklessness* is his first published book of prose. He is currently the William Livingston Chair in Poetry at the University of Texas at Austin.

The text of *The Art of Recklessness: Poetry as Assertive Force and Contradiction* is set in Warnock Pro, a typeface designed by Robert Slimbach for Adobe Systems in 2000. Book design by Wendy Holdman. Composition by BookMobile Design and Publishing Services, Minneapolis, Minnesota. Manufactured by Versa Press on acid-free paper.